日 対訳 英

ビジネスで使える英語のことわざ・名言 100

レベッカ・ミルナー＝著
ジェームス・M・バーダマン＝解説
宇野葉子＝日本語訳

INSPIRATIONAL PROVERBS AND
SAYINGS FOR BUSINESS

IBC PUBLISHING

装　　幀＝斉藤　啓
日本語訳＝宇野葉子
録　　音＝John Marshall Media, Educational

※ 本書の英文は、小社刊ラダーシリーズ『Inspirational Proverbs and Sayings（心に響く英語のことわざ・名言100)』から抜粋したものです。

本書を読むにあたって

　本書を手に取って、今まさに目を通されている方は、確実に英語が読めるようになりたいと思っているはずです。本書にたどり着いた方の中には、初めて英語の本を手にした方、何度も洋書に挑戦し挫折している方、何冊も買ってはいるけど読んでいない方など様々だと思います。あなたがこれまでどんな道をたどってきたとしても、是非本書との出会いを大切にしてほしいと思います。本文を読み始める前に少しだけ、僕がこれまでに何度も何度も繰り返し読んできたこの本のことについてお話しさせてください。飽きることなくどうして繰り返し読めたのか？　本書の何が僕をそこまで惹きつけたのか。

　本書のオリジナル版（Inspirational Proverbs and Sayings）を初めて手にした時、僕も英語が読めるようになりたくて、英語の本を探していました。飽きずに繰り返し読めて、適度に面白い英語の本はないかと。難し過ぎず、かと言って簡単過ぎず、そしてどこまでも自然な英語で書かれたもの……。そしてしばらく探した後、ついにこの本に出会ったのです。オリジナル版は対訳ではなかったのですが、読み始めてから僕の英語を読む感覚、もっと言うと英語に対する理解は大きく変わることになったのです。

飽きずに読める読み物との出会いは値千金
　英語を読めるようになるためにすべきこと、それは一言で言うと「読むこと」に他なりません。当たり前だと思われるかもしれませんが、読めるようになるためにすべきことは読むことなのです。飽きずに読める英語に出会えた人は、もう勝利のチケットを半分手にしたようなものなのです。

ことわざや名言ごとに、力強いメッセージが添えられた本書は、1日1つずつ読むだけでも、小さな一歩をこつこつと刻んでいける本なのです。やがて、その小さな一歩が大きな進歩につながっていたことに気づく日が必ず来るはずです。まずは無理せず、順番もどこからでも構いません、今日のあなたの好奇心の赴くままにページを開いてみましょう。

「英語は英語のままで」の本当の意味

　英語は英語のまま理解するのがやはりベストで、つまり英語がわかるというのは瞬時に日本語に訳せることではなく、Thank you. は Thank you. のまま、感謝されていることがわかるということに他なりません。ただ英語を英語のまま理解することの危険もあります。それは正しい理解ができているかのチェックが自分ではしづらいという点です。英語のまま理解するというのは、曖昧な理解のままでいい、ということではありません。その点、本書は対訳の日本語を通して自分の理解が正しいか、その場ですぐに確認できるようになっています。転ばないように補助輪がついた自転車のように、安心できる一冊なのです。一度日本語を読んで内容が理解できたら、後は日本語のグラデーションを落としていき、英語のままで意味を理解できるようにしていくことが大切です。補助輪はいつかは取るもの、そしてスピードを上げて自由に走り出すのです。

自然な英語を自分の中にインストールしていく感覚

　本書を読み始めると、知っている単語ばかりで書かれていることがわかると思います。ただ知っている単語ばかりなのに意味の取れないものや、日本語の発想では絶対に出てこない英語の表現が散りばめられていることにも気づくはずです。それこそが僕たちとネイティブの差であり、そこにこそ英語をインプットする上で大切なエッセンスが詰まっているのです。ネイティブが書いたどこまでも自然な英文の中にこそ、僕たちの感覚にはない英語が英語らしく輝きを放つ瞬間というものがあります。僕たちはその生きた英語を生きたまま味わい、心に刻んでいくことで英語の感覚をイ

ンストールできるのだと思います。栄養価が高く、フレッシュな食材のようなオーガニックな英語がこの本にはたくさん実っているのです。

「アクティブに読む」という感覚

　読むという行為はインプット行為なのですが、意識を変えることで限りなくアウトプットの要素を盛り込むこともできると僕は思っています。「片付け」は、片付けるという行為でもありながら、次に使う時のことを考えて片付けさえすれば、それは使う行為の準備にもなりうるわけです。言ってみたくなる言葉、使ってみたくなる言葉にあふれた本書は、そういう意味では常に使うことを頭の片隅に置きながら読むのに最適な本なのです。本書の隅から隅まで、言えたらいいな、サラッと言ってみたいな、という言葉が満載です。次に使う時のことをとことん考えながら頭の中に収納し、いつでも取り出しやすいようにインプットしてみましょう。使うことを意識しながら読む英語は、アウトプットするために口からスッと出やすいものです。それこそがアクティブに読むということなのです。「読むこと」が「話すこと」にも直結してくるのです。ただ漫然と読むのではなく、今度使ってみよう、という気持ちを常に持ちながら本書を読み進めてみてください。お気に入りの格言もきっと見つかるはず。それはいつか自分自身の言葉として、あなたの会話を鮮やかに彩ってくれるはずです。

いつも手を伸ばせば届くところに置いておく

　「よし！今日も英語の本を読もう」という気持ちは大事なのですが、もっと大事なのは気づいてたら読んでいた、そんなある意味ストレスフリーなスタンスです。英語が快適に読めるところにたどり着くまでには少し時間が必要です。そのためにはまず手を伸ばせば届くところにこの本を置いておきましょう。コーヒーを飲みながら、ベランダで日曜日の爽やかな風に吹かれながら、ベッドに入って夢の中に落ちていくその前に、気づけばあなたのそばにいつもいる友達のようにこの本をそばに置いてあげてください。英語を読むということが日々の営みの中に、自然にスッと入り込んで

くる、そんな瞬間が必ずやってくると思います。そうなれば「英語を読むぞ」、とそんな意気込みなんてなくても英語をストレスなくどんどん読めているはずです。

　本書を通して、しなやかに力強く、そして軽やかにずしりと心に響く、そんな言葉の数々をぜひ味わってみてください。力まず、意気込まず、肩の力を抜いてまずは1ページ目をめくってみてください。きっとこれから長くあなたの心の中に残る言葉が、あなたとの出会いを待っているはずです。さあ、今日から英語を読むことを習慣にしてみませんか？

　Today is the first day of the rest of your life. なのですから。きっと何かが変わり始めるはずです。

2016年5月
英語キュレーター
セレン

Contents

本書を読むにあたって　*3*

Success 🌸 成功

1. Nothing great was ever achieved without enthusiasm　*16*
情熱なくして偉業が達成されたことはない

2. Where there's a will, there's a way　*18*
意志ある所に道あり

3. Time is money　*20*
時は金なり

4. Fight fire with fire　*22*
毒を以て毒を制す（相手と同じ手で攻める）

5. Talk is cheap　*24*
言うは易し

6. It ain't over 'til it's over　*26*
勝敗は最後までわからない

7. Rome wasn't built in a day　*28*
ローマは一日にしてならず

8. Opportunity never knocks twice　*30*
チャンスは二度やってこない

9. Don't get mad, get even　*32*
怒るな、やり返せ

10. You can't argue with success　*34*
論より証拠

11. What goes up must come down　*36*
上がるものは必ず下がる

12. When the going gets tough, the tough get going　*38*
状況が厳しいときはタフな人が成功する

13 You play to win the game　*40*
　勝つために戦え

14 If you can't beat 'em, join 'em　*42*
　長い物には巻かれろ

15 There is no substitute for hard work　*44*
　勤勉に代わるものはない

16 The early bird catches the worm　*46*
　早起きは三文の徳（早くきた鳥は虫を捕まえる）

17 Success is getting what you want; happiness is wanting what you get　*48*
　成功は欲しいものを手に入れること、幸福は手に入るものを欲しがること

18 The squeaky wheel gets the grease　*50*
　主張すれば見返りを得られる

19 Actions speak louder than words　*52*
　口先よりも実践が大事

20 There are no gains without pains (No pain, no gain)　*54*
　苦労なくして得るものなし（ノーペイン・ノーゲイン）

21 If a thing is worth doing, it's worth doing well　*56*
　やるからには最善を尽くせ

22 If you can dream it, you can do it　*58*
　夢見ることができれば、それは実現できる

23 Two heads are better than one　*60*
　三人寄れば文殊の知恵

24 Strike while the iron is hot　*62*
　鉄は熱いうちに打て

25 There's always room at the top　*64*
　最上の地位はいつでも空いている

👑 進化する「ことわざ」を使いこなす！　*66*

Love & Friendships 愛と友情

26 Don't judge a book by its cover *72*
見掛けで判断してはいけない

27 Never mix business with pleasure *74*
遊びと仕事を混同するな

28 There are plenty of fish in the sea *76*
(恋人にふられても) いい人は、まだたくさんいる

29 Understanding is a two-way street *78*
理解とは双方向なものだ

30 It takes two to tango *80*
タンゴは一人では踊れない (責任は両方にある)

31 Love is blind *82*
恋は盲目

32 Time heals all wounds *84*
時はすべての傷を癒やす

33 It is not fair to ask of others what you are unwilling to do yourself *86*
あなたがやりたくないことを他人に頼むのは、フェアではありません

34 Treat others the way you would like to be treated *88*
自分にしてもらいたいことを人にしてあげなさい

35 Let sleeping dogs lie *90*
寝た子を起こすな

36 If you look for the bad in people, you'll surely find it *92*
もし人々の中に「悪」を探すなら、それは確実に見つかるだろう

37 Absence makes the heart grow fonder *94*
遠ざかるほど想いは募る

38 If you can't say anything nice, don't say anything at all *96*
もし良いことが言えないのであれば、何も言うな

39 Two's company, three's a crowd *98*
二人は仲間、三人は人込み

40 Misery loves company *100*
同病相憐れむ

41 Knowledge speaks, but wisdom listens *102*
知識はものを言う。だが知恵は耳を傾ける

42 Good fences make good neighbors *104*
親しき仲にも礼儀あり

43 Good friends are hard to find *106*
良い友達は見つけるのが難しい

♛ 進化する「ことわざ」を使いこなす！ *108*

Human Nature 🌸 人間の本性

44 The grass is always greener on the other side of the fence *114*
隣の庭の芝生はいつも青い

45 Hindsight is always 20-20 *116*
あと知恵はいつも完璧

46 Nobody is perfect *118*
完璧な人間などいない

47 Old habits die hard *120*
身についた習慣はなかなか変わらない

48 Nice guys finish last *122*
お人好しでは勝てない

49 Beauty is only skin deep *124*
美人も皮一重

50 Man cannot live on bread alone *126*
人はパンだけで生きるものではない

51 A person's a person no matter how small *128*
どんなに小さくても人は人

52 The apple doesn't fall far from the tree *130*
蛙の子は蛙（リンゴは木からあまり遠いところへは落ちない）

53 Hunger is the best sauce *132*
空腹は最上のソース

54　Most people are about as happy as they make their minds up to be　*134*
多くの人は自分が幸福になろうと決心した程度だけ幸福である

55　One man's trash is another man's treasure　*136*
捨てる神あれば拾う神あり

56　You are as old as you think you are　*138*
自分の信じた年齢が、自分の年齢となる

👑 進化する「ことわざ」を使いこなす！　*140*

Good Advice 良き助言

57　Don't count your chickens before they've hatched　*146*
捕らぬ狸の皮算用（卵がかえる前にニワトリの数を数えても意味がない）

58　If you don't like the heat, get out of the kitchen　*148*
仕事の苦しさに耐えられないなら、仕事を変えよ

59　Don't bite off more than you can chew　*150*
自分の能力以上のことをやろうとするな

60　Money doesn't grow on trees　*152*
金のなる木はない

61　Quit while you're ahead　*154*
勝っているうちにやめておけ

62　Don't bite the hand that feeds you　*156*
恩をあだで返すようなことはするな

63　People in glass houses shouldn't throw stones　*158*
ガラスの家に住む者は石を投げてはならない

64　Don't burn your bridges behind you　*160*
渡った橋を燃やしてしまうな

65　All that glitters is not gold　*162*
光るものすべてが金ではない

66　Be careful what you wish for　*164*
願い事をする時は気をつけなさい

67 What goes around, comes around　*166*
因果は巡る（自分の行いは自分に返ってくる）

68 The devil is in the details　*168*
悪魔は細部に宿る

69 If it ain't broke, don't fix it　*170*
壊れていないものを修理するな

70 Never say never　*172*
絶対にない、ということはない

71 Where there is smoke, there is fire　*174*
火のない所に煙は立たぬ

72 Don't put all your eggs in one basket　*176*
一つのことにすべてを賭けるな

73 Better safe than sorry　*178*
転ばぬ先の杖

74 What you don't know can't hurt you　*180*
知らぬが仏

👑 進化する「ことわざ」を使いこなす！　*182*

Lessons for Living 🌺 生きるための教訓

75 If life hands you a lemon, make lemonade　*188*
人生がレモンをくれるならそれでレモネードを作ればいい（つらい状況でも、ベストを尽くせ）

76 Today is the first day of the rest of your life　*190*
今日は残りの人生最初の日である

77 Don't sweat the small stuff　*192*
小さいことにくよくよするな

78 Truth is stranger than fiction　*194*
事実は小説よりも奇なり

79 Practice what you preach　*196*
人に説くことを自分でも実行しなさい

80 Every cloud has a silver lining *198*
どんな悪い状況でもどこかに希望があるものだ

81 Either get busy living or get busy dying *200*
精力的に生きるか、さもなくば慌ただしく死んでいくか

82 Beggars can't be choosers *202*
背に腹は代えられぬ（乞食はえり好みできない）

83 In the future everyone will be world-famous for fifteen minutes *204*
近い未来に、誰もが世界中で15分間有名になるだろう

84 You can't have your cake and eat it, too *206*
ケーキは食べたらなくなる

85 Wake up and smell the coffee *208*
ちゃんと目を覚まして現実を見なさい

86 Better late than never *210*
遅れても何もしないよりはまし

87 Anyone who has never made a mistake has never tried anything new *212*
間違いを犯したことのない人は、新しいことに挑戦したことがない人だ

88 What doesn't kill you only makes you stronger *214*
生きてさえいればどんな経験でも自分自身を強くする

89 Showing up is 80 percent of life *216*
顔見せは人生の80パーセント

90 There is no free lunch *218*
ただより高いものはない

91 It doesn't rain but it pours *220*
降れば土砂降り

92 A penny saved is a penny earned *222*
ちりも積もれば山となる

93 Control your own destiny, or someone else will *224*
自らの運命をコントロールせよ。さもなくば、他の誰かがそうするだろう

94 You don't need a weatherman to tell which way the wind blows *226*
風がどの方向に吹いているのか知るために、天気予報士は必要ない

95 When in Rome, do as the Romans do *228*
郷に入っては郷に従え

13

96 The only thing we have to fear is fear itself　*230*
私たちが恐れなければならない唯一のことは、恐れそのものである

97 Do a common thing in an uncommon way　*232*
普通ではない方法で普通のことをするのはすばらしいこと

98 Reality is something you rise above　*234*
現実とは踏み越えていくもの

99 There's no place like home　*236*
わが家にまさるところなし

100 The best things in life are free　*238*
人生で最も大切なものは、いくらお金を出しても手に入らない

👑 **進化する「ことわざ」を使いこなす！**　*240*

格言の著者　*244*

●付属 CD-ROM について●

　本書に付属のCD-ROMに収録されている音声は、パソコンや携帯音楽プレーヤーなどで再生することができるMP3ファイル形式です。パソコンのCD/DVDドライブに本ディスクを挿入して、iTunesなどの音楽再生（管理）ソフトにディスク内の音声ファイルを取り込んでご利用ください。
　一般的な音楽CDプレーヤーでは再生できませんので、ご注意ください。

■音楽再生・管理ソフトへの取り込みについて
　パソコンにMP3形式の音声ファイルに対応した音楽再生ソフトがインストールされていることをご確認ください。
　オーディオCDと異なり、本ディスクをCD/DVDドライブに入れただけでは、音楽再生ソフトは多くの場合自動的に起動しません。ご自分で音楽再生ソフトを直接起動して、「ファイル」メニューから「ライブラリに追加」したり、音楽再生ソフトのウインドウ上にファイルをマウスでドラッグ＆ドロップするなどして取り込んでください。
　音楽再生ソフトの詳しい操作方法や携帯音楽プレーヤー等へのファイルの転送方法については、ソフトやプレーヤーに付属のユーザーガイドやオンラインヘルプで確認するか、アプリケーションの開発元にお問い合わせください。

Success
成功

1

Nothing great was ever achieved without enthusiasm

Ralph Waldo Emerson, *author (1803–1882)*

情熱なくして偉業が達成されたことはない

ラルフ・ワルド・エマーソン
作家(1803〜1882)

Knowledge and skills can take you far in life, but they won't take you all the way. Enthusiasm takes you that extra step. Enthusiasm makes you excited about your work and your life. It makes you happy to get out of bed every morning.

Enthusiasm is the passion that we bring to our work. It is the difference between a good work of art and a great one. It is the difference between a good presentation and a great one. This is because enthusiasm has the power to inspire other people.

Knowledge and skills can be learned, but enthusiasm must come from inside. It comes naturally to a lucky few; others must look deep inside to discover it. Fortunately, enthusiasm spreads. Spend time with people who have passion, and their enthusiasm might spread to you.

....

知識と技能があれば、人生で成功できます。けれども、とことん成功することはできません。情熱があれば、さらに一歩進むことができます。仕事と生活に意欲的になれます。毎朝、起きるのがうれしくなります。

情熱とは仕事に注ぐ熱意のことです。情熱によって、良い芸術作品と偉大な芸術作品の違いが生まれます。良いプレゼンテーションと偉大なプレゼンテーションの違いが生まれます。なぜなら、情熱には人々を感動させる力があるからです。

知識と技能は学ぶことができますが、情熱は内面から生まれるものです。一部の幸運な人は生まれつき持っていますが、たいていの人は心の奥深くから見つけなければなりません。幸いにも、情熱は伝わります。熱意のある人といっしょにいれば、その人の情熱があなたにも伝わるかもしれません。

2

Where there's a will, there's a way

proverb

意志ある所に道あり

ことわざ

Some goals may seem impossible. However, if you are very determined, you can find a way to succeed.

Imagine you are standing at the edge of a forest. In front of you are thick trees. You can't see beyond the trees; however, you know that what you want is on the other side of the forest. The only problem is that there's no path. How are you going to get through? Will you give up and turn away? Or will you make your own path through the forest, even though you might get lost or hurt along the way?

If you are truly determined, you will make your own path. You will get to the other side no matter what; that is the power of determination.

・・・

到達できないと思われる目標もあります。けれども、固く決意すれば、成功の道を見つけることができます。

森の外れに立っているとします。目の前には木が生い茂っていて、まったく見通しがききません。けれども自分の求めるものが森の向こう側にあることはわかっています。ただ一つ問題なのは、道がないことです。あなたはどうやって切り抜けますか。あきらめて立ち去りますか。それとも、たとえ途中で迷ったり傷ついたりしても、自分で道をつくり森のなかを通り抜けようとしますか。

あなたの決意が本物なら、道をつくることができます。何が起ころうと森の向こう側に着くことができるでしょう。これこそ決意の力なのです。

19

3

Time is money

Ben Franklin, *author (1706–1790)*

時は金なり

ベンジャミン・フランクリン
文筆家(1706〜1790)

The number of hours in a day is limited to just twenty-four. If you waste time, you will be able to do less in those hours. The less you do, the less money you and your business can make. Move quickly and make decisions quickly to make the most of this time.

Ben Franklin said this over two hundred years ago; however, his words are even truer today. We move faster than before thanks to modern technology. We prefer airplanes to buses and emails to telephone calls. Buses are cheaper, but airplanes get us places faster. Telephone calls build good relationships, but emails take less time. With the time you save, you can work more—not that this is always a good thing!

・・

一日はほんの24時間です。無駄に使えば、この時間にできることが少なくなります。できることが少ないほど、あなたやあなたの会社の稼ぎは少なくなります。すばやく行動し、すぐに決断して、この時間を最大限に活用してください。

ベンジャミン・フランクリンがこれを言ったのは200年以上前ですが、この言葉は当時より現在にいっそう当てはまります。現代技術のおかげで、人々は以前より早く移動できるようになりました。人々はバスより飛行機を好み、電話よりEメールを好みます。バスのほうが安価ですが、飛行機は目的地に早く着きます。電話を使うと良い関係を築けますが、Eメールは時間がかかりません。節約した時間で、もっと働くことができます。ただし、これがいつもいいとは限りません！

4

Fight fire with fire

proverb

毒を以て毒を制す
（相手と同じ手で攻める）

ことわざ

F ight back with equal strength. Fight back with equal determination and skill. Many battles are not easily won. Some battles can become ugly, especially if the prize is worth a lot. The greater the value of the prize, the more difficult the battle for it will be. If you hope to win, you had better fight with everything you have.

A Did you see Jim talking to Lisa this morning?

B Yeah, he must have been saying something funny because she was laughing. I can't compete with a guy like Jim.

A Sure you can. But you can't expect Lisa to notice you if you don't even talk to her. Come on, *fight fire with fire*. I bet you can make her laugh, too, if you try.

・・・

反撃は、相手と同じ強さでしなさい。同じ決意と手法でしなさい。たやすく勝てる戦いは多くはありません。見苦しくなる戦いもあり、特に、褒美の価値が高いとそうなりやすいです。褒美の価値が高いほど、それを得るための戦いが困難になります。勝ちたいと望むなら、持っているものすべてを使って戦うことです。

A 今朝、ジムがリサに話しかけているのを見たかい？

B ああ、あいつ何か面白いことを言ったに違いない。だって、彼女笑っていたからね。ジムのようなやつには勝てそうもない。

A きっと勝てるさ。だけど、話しかけてもいないのにリサがきみに気づいてくれると期待しちゃいけない。元気出せよ、相手と同じ手で攻めるんだ。きっときみだって彼女を笑わすことができるさ。ただしやってみたらの話だよ。

5

Talk is cheap

proverb

言うは易し

ことわざ

Talking about something is easy. Talking doesn't cost anything. Doing something takes more effort. It can take time and money, too.

Just because someone says something that doesn't mean he or she will actually do it. "Saying and doing are two different things" is another proverb that expresses this idea. There is also: "Easier said than done." Since there are several sayings that express this idea, it is clearly an important one to Americans!

Surely you can think of at least one person you know who often says things that he or she doesn't actually do. Maybe this person is you! Give him or her a little reminder that "saying and doing are two different things." "Talk is cheap" is a little more direct and is used between close friends.

・・

何かを話すことは簡単です。話すだけなら何もいりません。何かを実行するにはもっと努力が必要です。時間とお金も必要になります。

誰かが何かを言ったからって、その人が実際に実行するということではありません。「言うことと行うことは別である」ということわざも、この考えを表しています。ほかにも「言うは易く行うは難し」ということわざもあります。この考えを表すことわざがいくつもあることから、これがアメリカ人にとって重要なことは明らかです。

きっとあなたの周りにも、実行していないことをたびたび話す人が少なくとも一人はいるでしょう。それはあなたかもしれませんね。その人に「言うことと行うことは別である」ことをちょっと思い出させてあげてください。「言うは易し」というのは少し直接的な言い方で、親友同士で使われます。

6

It ain't over 'til it's over

Yogi Berra, *baseball player & manager (1925–2015)*

勝敗は最後までわからない

ヨギ・ベラ

野球選手・監督(1925〜2015)

P icture this: the score is 7 to 4 and the baseball game is almost over. The losing team doesn't have a chance, right? Now it is time for the last batter. The bases are loaded. He hits the ball out of the park. It's a grand slam and the game finishes 7 to 8.

A lot can happen between "almost over" and "over." It is important to keep trying until the very end. Anything is possible!

A Look at the score. I don't have a chance. I should just go home.

B Hey, don't give up! After all, *it ain't over 'til it's over.*

こんな場面を想像してください。得点は7対4、野球の試合はほぼ終わろうとしています。負けているチームにチャンスはなさそうですよね。さて、ラストバッターの登場です。塁は埋まっています。バッターは場外ホームランを打ちました。満塁ホームランで、試合は7対8で終了。

「ほぼ終わり」と「終わり」のあいだで、たくさんのことが起こり得ます。大切なのは、最後の最後まで挑戦し続けることです。何だって起こる可能性があるのですから。

A 得点を見ろよ。ぼくにはチャンスがない。もう家に帰ることにするよ。

B おい、あきらめるなよ。何と言っても、勝敗は最後までわからないからね。

7

Rome wasn't built in a day

proverb

ローマは一日にしてならず

ことわざ

Great things take time to create. Great things also take hard work. Rome was one of the greatest cities in Western history. However, it took hundreds of years and hundreds of small steps to become great. Great books take years to write; a successful career can take decades to create.

There will also be challenges along the way. It is important to stay positive, be patient, and keep your eyes on the goal.

A How is your business doing?

B It's doing okay. I just don't seem to be making much progress. I thought I'd have a big office by now. I thought I'd have people working for me.

A You will, someday. Those things just take time. Remember that *Rome wasn't built in a day*.

B That's what everyone keeps telling me.

・・・

偉大なものをつくるには時間がかかります。厳しい労働も必要です。ローマは西洋史のなかで最も偉大な都市の一つです。けれども、何百年もかけて何百もの小さな歩みを重ねて偉大になったのです。偉大な本を書くには何年もかかり、立派な経歴をつくるには何十年もかかるのです。

もちろん、途中で難問にぶつかることもあるでしょう。大切なのは、いつも前向きで、我慢をして、目標を見据えることです。

A 仕事の具合はどうだい？

B うまくいっている。ただ、大きな進歩がないように感じる。今ごろには大きなオフィスが持てると思っていたのにね。それに部下も持てると思っていたよ。

A きっといつかそうなるよ。そういうことには時間がかかるんだ。「ローマは一日にしてならず」って言うじゃないか。

B みんなぼくにそう言うよ。

8

Opportunity never knocks twice

proverb

チャンスは二度やってこない

ことわざ

When an opportunity comes, take it. Another one might not come for a long time. Another one might never come.

It is lucky when opportunity knocks on your door. Unfortunately, opportunity sometimes comes at the wrong time. Often, it comes before you are ready for it. When this happens, it is easy to think, "I will wait for a better time." However, a better time might not come. This might be your only chance, so don't miss it. Next time, opportunity might knock on your friend's door or your neighbor's door instead.

A I got offered a new job.
B Hey, that's great!
A Yeah, the position is great. The pay is great. The only problem is that I would have to move to London. I just moved into a new apartment here. I don't want to move again…
B Hey, *opportunity doesn't knock twice*! You should take the job.

チャンスがきたら、つかみなさい。次のチャンスがくるまで長い時間がかかるかもしれません。チャンスはもうこないかもしれません。

チャンスが訪れるのは幸運なことです。困ったことに、チャンスは都合の悪いときに訪れることもあります。たいてい、準備ができる前です。そんな時、「もっと良い時期まで待とう」と考えがちです。けれども、良い時期はこないかもしれません。今回が唯一のチャンスかもしれないので、決して逃してはなりません。次は、チャンスはあなたではなく、友人や隣人に訪れるかもしれないのです。

A 新しい仕事を勧められたんだ。
B へえ、すごいね。
A そうなんだ。地位もいいし、給料も高い。ただ問題なのは、ロンドンに引っ越さないといけないことだ。ちょうどここの新しいアパートに引っ越したばかりで、また動きたくないんだ……。
B なあ、チャンスは二度やってこないよ。その仕事を引き受けるべきだよ。

9

Don't get mad, get even

Joseph P. Kennedy, *businessman and politician*
(1888–1969)

怒るな、やり返せ

ジョセフ・P・ケネディ
実業家・政治家(1888〜1969)

Joseph P. Kennedy was the father of John F. Kennedy, the 35th president of the United States. He was also a very successful businessman, so he certainly knew about getting ahead! Kennedy may not have been the first person to say, "Don't get mad, get even," but he made the saying famous.

To get even means to get revenge. It is not very kind advice, but there is some truth to it. Anger is a waste of energy; it won't take you anywhere. Instead, turn your anger into action. Action is a lot more likely to help you get ahead. When under control, anger can actually be excellent motivation. The secret is to keep it under control and to use it for good.

ジョセフ・P・ケネディは、第35代アメリカ合衆国大統領ジョン・F・ケネディの父親です。実業家としても成功を収めたので、きっと出世する方法を知っていたのでしょう。初めて「怒るな、やり返せ」と言ったのはケネディではなかったかもしれませんが、彼がこの言葉を有名にしました。

やり返せというのは復讐しろということです。あまり親切な助言とは言えないかもしれませんが、真実も含まれています。怒りはエネルギーの無駄づかいで、あなたをどこにも導いてくれません。そんなことより、怒りを行動に変えなさい。行動は成功をあと押ししてくれる可能性が高いのです。抑えることさえできれば、怒りは実際に意欲を高めてくれます。秘訣は、常に怒りを抑えそれを良いことに使うことです。

10

You can't argue with success

proverb

論より証拠

ことわざ

Success often doesn't make sense. It can be hard to understand why some products sell millions while others don't. It can be even harder to understand why some people are successful while others aren't. A product can be useless but still a success. A person can be very nice but not a success at all. Unfortunately, in the world of business, it is the success part that matters the most. Even if you don't like someone or something, if it is successful then it is hard to argue against it.

A I can't believe you did that. Don't you think that was a little, uh, unkind?

B It worked, didn't it? And *you can't argue with success*, right?

・・・

成功の意味がわからなくなることがたびたびあります。何百万も売れる製品がある一方で売れない製品があることを理解するのは難しい。成功する人がいる一方でそうでない人がいることは、なおさら理解しにくい。製品が役に立たなくても、それでも成功なのです。人物がすばらしくても、成功したとはまったく言えないこともあります。残念なことに、ビジネスの世界で一番問題になるのは成功するかどうかです。たとえ人物やものを好きになれなくても、成功しているものに対して異議を唱えることは難しいのです。

A あなたがこんなことするなんて信じられない。少し、うーん、不親切だとは思わなかったの？

B それでうまくいったじゃないか。論より証拠だよ。

11

What goes up must come down

proverb

上がるものは必ず下がる

ことわざ

If you throw a ball into the air, it will fall back down. This is the law of nature. An airplane can't stay in the sky forever.

Someone who rises will also probably fall. It is unusual for a person to stay successful for a long time. Think of an actress who was very popular ten years ago. Is she still as popular now? Probably she isn't. Somebody new will have taken her place at the top.

It's not just people, though. Companies or even countries that are powerful today weren't always so powerful. Some that aren't powerful now used to be very powerful. Getting to the top doesn't mean that you get to stay at the top forever. Everything and everyone come down eventually.

空中にボールを投げれば、落ちてきます。これは自然の法則です。飛行機はずっと空中に留まることはできません。

高い地位についている人もおそらくそこから落ちるでしょう。人が長期にわたって成功しているなんて、普通ではありません。例えば、10年前にとても人気のあった女優のことを考えてください。彼女は今も同じように人気がありますか。たぶんそうではないでしょう。新人が彼女の代わりにトップの位置にいるでしょう。

ところが、これは人についてだけの話ではありません。今日、力のある会社、いえ国さえもが、必ずしもそんなに力があったわけではありません。現在、力のないものが昔はとても力があったこともあります。トップの地位についても、いつまでもそこにいられるわけではありません。すべてのもの、すべての人は、いつかは落ちるのです。

12

When the going gets tough, the tough get going

Frank Leahy, *football coach (1908–1973)*

状況が厳しいときはタフな人が成功する

フランク・リーヒー

フットボールコーチ(1908〜1973)

Difficult times are a test of strength. Being able to survive a difficult situation is evidence of strength.

If you're in a difficult situation, don't feel bad about yourself. Instead, see the situation as a chance to show your strength. A difficult situation is simply a challenge and an opportunity to grow stronger.

It is better to practice against a strong team than a weak team. If you win, you'll feel great; however, even if you lose, you will have learned something from the experience. The same is true in business and life in general: bad times push us to be stronger and to work harder. Don't miss these opportunities to show how tough you really are. You might even surprise yourself!

....

困難な時期には強さが試されます。困難な状況を乗り越えることができれば、強さの証になります。

困難な状況に陥ったとき、自分を嫌にならないでください。その代わり、その状況を自分の強さを試す機会だと思ってください。困難な状況は単に挑戦であり、強くなるための機会なのです。

弱いチームより強いチームと練習するほうが効果的です。勝つことができれば気分が良くなります。たとえ負けても、その経験から何かを学ぶことができます。これは一般にビジネスや人生においても言えます。つらい時期は、強くなって一生懸命働くようにわたしたちをあと押ししてくれます。この機会を逃さずに、あなたがいかにタフであるか示してください。自分でも驚くかもしれませんよ！

13

You play to win the game

Herman Edwards, *football player & coach (1954–)*

勝つために戦え

ハーマン・エドワーズ
フットボール選手・コーチ(1954〜)

If you're not playing to win, why are you playing? If you are not trying your hardest, why try at all? Playing is fun, but it is the goal of winning that makes a game what it is. Winning isn't only about sports. You can often hear Americans say "life is a game."

Of course, winning "the game of life" means different things to different people. It doesn't have to mean making the most money or earning the highest position. Winning can mean whatever you want it to mean, so long as you set goals and work to achieve them. It is important to decide what winning means to you. Then, once you've decided, go after what you want!

・・・

勝つために戦わないのなら、なぜ戦うのですか。最善を尽くそうとしないなら、そもそもなぜ戦おうとするのですか。戦いは面白いかもしれませんが、試合を試合足らしめているのは勝つという目標です。勝つことはスポーツに限りません。「人生はゲームだ」とアメリカ人はよく言います。

もちろん、「人生というゲーム」に勝つことは、人によって意味が違います。必ずしも大金を稼ぐことや最高の地位につくことではありません。勝つ対象は、目標を定めそれを得るために努力している限り、意味があると思うものであれば何でもいいのです。大切なのは、あなたにとって勝つことが何を意味するか見極めることです。いったん見極めたら、望みのものを目指してください。

14

If you can't beat 'em, join 'em

proverb

長い物には巻かれろ

ことわざ

If you're on the losing side, take a look at the winners. They must be doing something right. It would be a good idea to learn from them. It might even be a good idea to work with them—to join them. Don't be so stubborn as to miss a chance to learn something or to get ahead.

A Wow, you look nice. Did you get a haircut?

B Yeah. The suit is new, too.

A Since when did you start caring about the way you look?

B I don't care about the way I look. But I've noticed that women pay more attention to guys who care about the way they look.

A Ah, I get it. *If you can't beat 'em, join 'em.*

B Exactly!

・・

もし敗者の立場にいるなら、ちらっと勝者を見てください。勝者は何か正しいことをしているはずです。彼らから学ぶというのはいい考えです。彼らといっしょに行動し、彼らに加わるのはもっといい考えです。意固地になって、何かを学ぶ機会や成功する機会を失わないでください。

A うわーっ、格好いいじゃないか。髪を切ったの？

B ああ、スーツも新調だよ。

A いつから身なりに気をつけるようになったんだい？

B 身なりに気をつけているわけじゃない。だけど、女性が身なりに気をつけるやつのほうに関心があることに気づいたんだ。

A そうなのか。長い物には巻かれろだな。

B その通りさ。

15

There is no substitute for hard work

Thomas Edison, *inventor (1847–1931)*

勤勉に代わるものはない

トーマス・エジソン
発明家(1847〜1931)

Hard work is always an important part of success. This is true no matter how talented, attractive, rich, or popular you are. It's not what you are born with, but how you use it that really matters.

It is easy to look at a famous athlete and think: "He is successful because he has natural talent." You might say something similar about a famous actress: "She is successful because she is beautiful." However, talent and beauty are only a part of success. Even naturally talented athletes and beautiful actresses have to work hard. Talent doesn't mean a baseball player doesn't have to practice. Beauty doesn't mean that an actress doesn't have to remember her lines.

Talent and beauty can help you get ahead, but they aren't everything. Hard work is always neccessary.

成功には勤勉がつきものです。どんなに才能があり、魅力があり、お金があり、人気があっても同じです。本当に大事なのは持って生まれたものではなく、それをどのように使うかということです。

有名な運動選手を見ると、「持って生まれた才能があるから成功したんだ」と考えがちです。同じようなことを有名女優についても言うかもしれません。「美しいから成功したんだ」と。けれども、才能や美しさは成功の一部に過ぎません。生まれつき才能がある運動選手や美しい女優でさえ、勤勉にならないといけないのです。才能があるからといって、野球選手が練習しなくていいわけではありません。美しいからといって、女優がせりふを覚えなくていいわけではありません。

才能と美しさは成功をあと押しすることはできますが、それらがすべてではありません。常に必要とされるのは勤勉なのです。

16

The early bird catches the worm

proverb

早起きは三文の徳
（早くきた鳥は虫を捕まえる）

ことわざ

When you see an opportunity, act quickly. If you wait too long, someone else will get it before you. This is especially true in the fast-moving world of business. It can also be true in love: if you wait too long to tell someone how you feel, you might lose your chance.

In America, you might see restaurants selling "early bird specials." It doesn't mean they are selling worms! It's a special low price for customers who eat early, usually between 4 p.m. and 6 p.m., before the restaurant becomes busy.

A Did you hear that Linda is leaving the company? That means a new senior management position will be opening up…

B I've already handed in my resume.

A That was fast!

B You know what they say, *the early bird catches the worm*.

機会を見つければ、すぐに行動しなさい。長く待ちすぎると、誰かに先を越されるかもしれません。このことは動きの早いビジネスの世界に特に当てはまります。愛についても当てはまります。自分の気持ちをいつまでも相手に打ち明けずにいると、機会を逃すかもしれません。

アメリカには「早くきた人（鳥）スペシャル」を売り物にしているレストランがありますが、虫を売っているわけではありません！　レストランが忙しくなる前のたいてい午後の４時から６時のあいだにくる客に特別割引することを意味します。

A リンダが会社をやめるって聞いた？　それって、新しい管理職のポストが空くってこと……。

B もう履歴書を提出したわ。

A なんと早いこと！

B 「早起きは三文の徳」って言うじゃないの。

47

17

Success is getting what you want; happiness is wanting what you get

Dale Carnegie, *businessman & author (1888–1955)*

成功は欲しいものを手に入れること、幸福は手に入るものを欲しがること

デール・カーネギー
実業家・著述家(1888〜1955)

What does success mean to you? Does it mean money or a job at a famous company? Does it mean living in a particular neighborhood or driving a particular type of car? Will getting those things actually make you happy?

Think about the things—and people—that really do make you happy. Are these the same things that you think about when you think about success? If so, you can think of yourself as lucky! If not, maybe you need to change your ideas about success. Success and happiness should go together. For this to happen, you need to have a clear idea of what makes you happy—and a clear idea of how to get it.

・・・

あなたにとって成功とは何でしょう。お金持ちになることあるいは有名な会社で働くことですか。特別な地域で暮らすことあるいは特別なタイプの車を運転することですか。そのようなものを手に入れたら本当に幸せになれますか。

あなたを本当に幸せにしてくれるものや人々について考えてください。あなたが成功について考えたときと同じものですか。そうなら、あなたは幸運です。そうでないなら、成功に対する考えを変えたほうがいいかもしれません。成功と幸せは調和していなければなりません。そのためには、自分を幸せにしてくれるものと、それを得る方法について明確な考えを持つ必要があります。

18

The squeaky wheel gets the grease

proverb

主張すれば見返りを得られる

ことわざ

Imagine walking into a café on a cold day. You order a hot chocolate to warm up. However, when the hot chocolate arrives, it isn't very hot at all. What do you do? Do you drink the hot chocolate, even though it isn't hot? Or do you complain and ask for another one, one that is actually hot enough to warm you up?

If you don't complain, you won't get what you want. If you do complain, you will.

The wheel that is making noise will get the grease that it needs. The person who speaks up gets what he or she wants. If you want something, you have to let people know that you want it. If you don't tell someone, how will they know?

・・

寒い日にカフェに入ったと想像してください。ホットチョコレートを注文して体を温めようとします。ところが、ホットチョコレートが運ばれてくると、まったく熱くありません。あなたはどうしますか。熱くなくても飲みますか。それとも、文句を言って、体を温めるのに十分熱いものに取り替えてもらいますか。

文句を言わなければ欲しいものを手に入れることはできません。文句を言えばできます。

うるさい音を立てる車輪は必要な油を差してもらえます。欲しいと主張する人は欲しいものを手に入れることができます。何かが欲しいなら、そのことをほかの人に知ってもらわなければなりません。誰にも言わなければ、どうしてわかってもらえるでしょう。

51

19

Actions speak louder than words

proverb

口先よりも実践が大事

ことわざ

What you do has more power than what you say. Use actions instead of words when you really want someone to notice you.

Here's an example: Joe and Amy are friends. Joe likes Amy, but Amy doesn't know it. Joe often says nice things to Amy. He tells her that she is kind and pretty. But Amy really is kind and pretty, so lots of people tell her this. When Joe says it, Amy doesn't even notice. One day Joe decides to send Amy flowers. Now she notices him! Now she knows that he likes her.

Since actions do get noticed though, be extra careful with what you do. Once you've done something, you can't undo it.

・・・

行動はものを言うより力があります。誰かに自分のことを本当に気づいてもらいたいなら、言葉ではなく行動で示しなさい。

例を挙げましょう。ジョーとエイミーは友人同士です。ジョーはエイミーのことが好きなのに、エイミーは気づいていません。ジョーはいつもエイミーにすてきな言葉をかけ、「きみは親切でかわいい」と言っています。ところが、エイミーは本当に親切でかわいいので、たくさんの人にそう言われています。ジョーにそう言われても、気づいてさえいません。ある日、ジョーはエイミーに花を送ることにしました。やっとエイミーは彼に気づきました。ようやく彼が自分を好きだということを知ったのです。

とはいえ行動は相手に気づいてもらいやすいので、自分のすることには特に注意しなければなりません。いったん行動を起こすと、元に戻すことができないからです。

20

There are no gains without pains (No pain, no gain)

Ben Franklin, *author (1706–1790)*

苦労なくして得るものなし
(ノーペイン・ノーゲイン)

ベンジャミン・フランクリン
文筆家(1706〜1790)

These days the shorter saying, "no pain, no gain," is more common than Ben Franklin's original expression.

"No pain, no gain" is particularly popular in the sports world. Athletes often practice so hard that their whole body hurts. However, this practice has a purpose: it is supposed to make them stronger, better players. Unless they feel this pain, the coach may say, they are not practicing hard enough.

People use this saying in ordinary life, too. Sometimes if you want to succeed, you have to push yourself hard. This could mean staying up all night to study or working long after it is time to go home. Just remember that there is a limit!

・・

最近は短い言い方の「ノーペイン・ノーゲイン」がベンジャミン・フランクリンの元の表現より一般的です。

「ノーペイン・ノーゲイン」は特にスポーツ界で好まれています。運動選手は厳しい練習をすることが多いので、体全体が痛みます。けれども、この練習には目的があり、もっと強く、もっと優れた選手になることが期待されています。選手がこの痛みを感じなければ、コーチに厳しい練習が不十分だと言われるかもしれません。

このことわざは普通の生活でも使われます。成功したければ、時にはかなり無理をしなければなりません。例えば、徹夜で勉強することや、長時間残業することです。でも、それにも限度があることを忘れないでください！

21

If a thing is worth doing, it's worth doing well

proverb

やるからには最善を尽くせ

ことわざ

If you are going to take the time and energy to do something, do it well. Do the best that you can. If you're not going to do it well, why do it at all? Doing something poorly is a waste of time and energy. Do a thing well so that you can be proud of it.

A Have you finished practicing the piano already?
B I practiced for half an hour. I'll practice more tomorrow.
A Don't you like playing the piano?
B I do like it…
A Then you should keep practicing. *If a thing is worth doing, it's worth doing well.*

時間と労力をかけて何かをするなら、しっかりやりなさい。最善を尽くすのです。最善を尽くそうとしないのなら、そもそもどうしてするのですか。いい加減にすることは時間と労力の無駄づかいです。最善を尽くして、やったことを誇れるようになってください。

A もうピアノの練習は終わり？
B 30分やったわ。明日はもっとするつもり。
A ピアノを弾くのが好きじゃないの？
B 好きだけれど……。
A それなら、もっと練習しなさい。「やるからには最善を尽くせ」って言うでしょ。

22

If you can dream it, you can do it

Walt Disney, *filmmaker & businessman (1901–1966)*

夢見ることができれば、それは実現できる

ウォルト・ディズニー
映画製作者・実業家(1901~1966)

People used to say "the sky is the limit." This meant that anything on Earth was possible. People used to dream about airplanes. Now they really exist. Now we also have rockets. Clearly the sky is no longer the limit. Now the whole universe is open to us.

Don't limit yourself to what you think is possible. What is possible is always changing. The dreams of ordinary people are largely responsible for this change. Let yourself dream. Let your dreams open your mind to a whole different world—a world where anything is possible. Then think about how you can turn your dreams into reality.

・・・

以前は「可能性は無限大」という言葉をよく耳にしました。これは地球上では何事も可能だという意味です。昔、人々は飛行機を夢見ましたが、今は実現しています。ロケットだってあります。明らかに、空にはもう制限はありません。今や人類には宇宙全体が開かれています。

自分が可能だと思うものだけに自分自身を制限しないでください。可能なものはいつも変化しています。たいてい、普通の人々の夢がこの変化をもたらすのです。さあ、夢見てください。夢を見てまったく違う世界に――どんなことだって起こり得る世界に――心を開きましょう。そして、どのようにすれば自分の夢を実現できるか考えてください。

23

Two heads are better than one

proverb

三人寄れば文殊の知恵

ことわざ

Two people working together will do a better job than just one person working alone. This is because every person has his or her own strong points and weak points. One person's weak point may be the other person's strong point. Two people working together will have the shared strong points of both people. Having two people work together also means having more ideas.

Having two people work together is a good thing. Having lots of people work together can create problems. This is because there will be too many different ideas and different personalities. There is another proverb to describe this situation: "Too many cooks spoil the soup."

  A Do you need any help?

  B Sure, that would be great. *Two heads are better than one.*

・・・

二人で働くほうがたった一人で働くより良い仕事ができます。なぜかというと、人にはそれぞれ強みと弱みがあるからです。一人の弱みがもう一人の強みになるかもしれません。二人で働くと両者の強みを分かち合えるでしょう。二人で働くと、もっと多くのことを思いつくこともできるでしょう。

二人で働くのはすばらしいことです。たくさんの人と働くと問題が起こることがあります。なぜかというと、考えの違いや個性の違いが多くなり過ぎるからです。この様子を表現することわざに「船頭多くして船山に登る」があります。

  A 手伝いましょうか？

  B ええ、助かります。三人寄れば文殊の知恵ですからね。

61

24

Strike while the iron is hot

proverb

鉄は熱いうちに打て

ことわざ

This is your chance to do something, so don't miss it. Act now, or you may not have the chance to act again.

It is often said that "timing is everything." A good plan may fail because it is introduced at the wrong time. An ordinary plan might succeed, just because the timing is right. Unfortunately timing is usually out of your control. The right timing may come before you are ready for it or when you don't expect it. Always be prepared so that you can act when the right time comes.

A Did you talk to the boss about your raise?
B No, not yet.
A He's in a really good mood today. You should talk to him.
B I don't know. I haven't thought about what to say yet…
A He's not in a good mood very often. I'd *strike while the iron is hot* and talk to him now.

・・

何かをする機会が訪れたとき、それを逃してはなりません。すぐに行動しないと、二度とそんな機会はこないかもしれません。

「何事もタイミング」とよく言われます。すばらしい計画も始めるタイミングが悪ければ失敗するかもしれません。平凡な計画もタイミングが良いというだけで成功することがあります。残念ながら、普通はタイミングを制御することはできません。良いタイミングが、準備する前や思いがけない時に訪れるかもしれません。いつも準備して、良いタイミングがきた時に行動できるようにしましょう。

A 昇給のこと、ボスに話したかい？
B まだなんだ。
A 今日はボスの機嫌がすごくいいよ。話すべきだよ。
B そう言われてもなあ。どう言うかまだ考えていないし……。
A ボスの機嫌がいい時はめったにない。ぼくなら今話すね。「鉄は熱いうちに打て」って言うだろ。

25

There's always room at the top

Daniel Webster, *lawyer & politician (1782–1852)*

最上の地位はいつでも空いている

ダニエル・ウェブスター
法律家・政治家(1782〜1852)

Daniel Webster was one of the most famous lawyers in American history. A young law student once complained to him that there were no good jobs for young people. To this Webster replied, "There's always room at the top."

Webster's advice is this: If you are the best at what you do, there will always be a job for you. The best way to make sure that you will have a job is to become very good at what you do. Aim for the top. Even if you don't make it, you will have tried your hardest.

A I'm going to study law.

B Really? There are already too many lawyers. Aren't you worried about finding a job?

A Not at all. *There's always room at the top.*

ダニエル・ウェブスターはアメリカ史で最も有名な弁護士の一人です。かつて若い法学部の学生が、若者にはいい仕事がないと彼に不満を言いました。これに対してウェブスターは、「最上の地位はいつでも空いているものだ」と答えました。

ウェブスターの助言の意味はこうです。自分の関わっている分野で最も優秀であれば、常に仕事がある。確実に仕事につく最良の方法は、自分の関わっている分野を得意になること。一番を目指せ。たとえうまくいかなくても、できるだけのことはしたことになる。

A 法律を学ぼうと思う。

B そうなの？　今だって法律家は山ほどいるわよ。職につけるか心配じゃないの？

A そんなことないよ。最上の地位はいつでも空いているからね。

Success

"Time is money" has been applied to America and its people to describe the importance of capitalism in that society. The proverb has an unpleasant ring to more people these days, perhaps because they think that "time" is not a commodity and that having "free time" is irreplaceable. Rather than this particular proverb, many would prefer to say, "Time is precious," which means that time is valuable in many ways, as an opportunity for leisure or as something to be treated with care in the workplace. Because many people's lives have become so busy that they seem to always be working, we often recommend something such as "take time to smell the roses." This of course means that no matter how busy we seem to be, we should take a few minutes here and there to remember what is important in life. Enjoy life rather than just being busy all the time.

One of the best of the proverbs reverses words and contains wisdom we all can recognize: "Success is getting what you want; happiness is wanting what you get." In

進化する「ことわざ」を使いこなす！

成功

「時は金なり」とはアメリカという国家やアメリカ人に当てはめられた言葉で、アメリカ社会における資本主義の重要性を表しています。最近、このことわざに対して不快に思う人たちが増えてきました。それはおそらく、「時間」とは商品ではなく、「自由時間」を持つことはかけがえのないことだというふうに考えるようになったからでしょう。この決まり切ったことわざよりも、「時は貴重である」というほうを好む人が多くなっています。つまり、余暇として、仕事場で大事にされるべきものとして、あらゆる点で時間には価値があるということを意味しているのです。多くの人たちの生活は忙しさが増し、いつも働いているような状態です。だからこそ、「バラの香りをかぐ時間を持ちなさい」というようなことがよく推奨されるようになったのです。もちろん、この一文が意味するのは、どんなに忙しくても、時々、人生で大切なものは何かを思い浮かべる時間を持たなければならないということです。四六時中忙しくしているよりも、人生を楽しんではいかがですか。

最高のことわざの一つに、言葉の意味を裏返し、すべての人たちが理解できる英知を含んでいるものがあります。すなわち、「成功とは望むものを手にすることであり、幸せとは手にあるものを望むことである」。言い換えると、成功とは人を幸せにするものではな

other words, success is not what makes you happy. True happiness comes from being content with whatever you have.

"The squeaky wheel gets the grease" is an old proverb that comes from the days of wagons with wheels and although we know what it means, English speaker would rather replace it with something like "those who complain get attention first."

Most of the proverbs of success emphasize the importance of devotion and continuity. "There is no substitute for hard work," "No pain, no gain," and the playfully expressed "When the going gets tough, the tough get going" all stress the importance of not giving up. Instead, one has to put more effort into what one does.

進化する「ことわざ」を使いこなす!

いのです。本当の幸せは、あなたが得たものが何であろうと、それに満足しているときに感じられるのです。

「きしむ車輪は油を差される」とは古い言い回しで、車輪付きの荷馬車が引かれた時代のものですが、今の時代でもその言わんとするところは理解できます。英語で言い換えるならば、「不平を言う人は最初に注目される」という感じでしょうか。

成功を表すことわざのほとんどは、献身と継続の重要性を強調します。「勤勉に代わるものはない」、「苦労なくして得るものはなし」、そしておどけた感じで表現された「状況が厳しいときはタフな人が成功する」といったこれらのことわざもすべて、あきらめないことの大切さを強調しています。それよりも、やるときには、もっと努力することです。

Love & Friendships

愛と友情

26

Don't judge a book by its cover

proverb

見掛けで判断してはいけない

ことわざ

What you see is not always what you get. Book covers can look boring or interesting, but you won't know the truth about the book until you read it. Glasses can make a person look smart. A rich man may wear simple clothes. A sad person may laugh and smile. You can't really know people just by looking at them. Inside, they could be completely different.

- **A** Did you see the new guy?
- **B** Yeah. He looks really serious.
- **A** Have you talked to him?
- **B** No, not yet. But have you noticed that he never smiles?
- **A** Maybe he's just shy. *Don't judge a book by its cover.*
- **B** Yeah, you're right. Have you talked to him?
- **A** No, I haven't either. Let's go introduce ourselves now.

・・・

見掛けと中身は必ずしも同じではありません。本の表紙が退屈そうにまたは面白そうに見えても、本当はどうなのかわかるのは読んでからです。眼鏡をかけると、人は賢そうに見えます。裕福な人が質素な服を着ているかもしれません。悲しい思いをしている人が笑い声を上げ、ほほえんでいるかもしれません。見掛けだけでは人のことを本当に知ることはできません。中身はまったく違うこともあります。

- **A** あの新人を見たかい？
- **B** ああ。彼はとても真面目そうだ。
- **A** 話したことはあるのかい？
- **B** いや、まだない。だけど、決して笑顔を見せないことに気がついた？
- **A** たぶん、恥ずかしいだけかもしれない。見掛けで判断してはいけないよ。
- **B** ああ、きみの言う通りだ。きみはあいつと話したのかい？
- **A** ぼくもまだだ。さあ、自己紹介しに行くか。

27

Never mix business with pleasure

proverb

遊びと仕事を混同するな

ことわざ

I t is better to keep relationships and work separate. Mixing the two—even though you might really want to—can lead to trouble.

Here's a common situation: there is a good-looking man or woman in your office. You want to get to know him or her, right? Maybe you start dating. At first things go well, but eventually you start fighting and break up. Now you never want to see that person again. The only problem is, you work in the same office so you'll have to meet every day. This stressful situation will likely affect your ability to work.

The other way around isn't a good idea either: friends and couples who start working together often have problems. Fights about money or ideas create negative feelings that can hurt relationships.

・・・

人間関係と仕事は別にしておくのが賢明です。二つを混ぜると、たとえ真剣にそうしたいと望んでも、問題が起こることがあります。

一般的な例を挙げましょう。あなたの職場に一人の顔立ちの良い男性か女性がいるとします。その人と知り合いになりたいと思いますよね。デートをするかもしれません。最初はうまくいきますが、そのうち喧嘩が始まり、別れることになります。そうなると、その人を二度と見たくなくなります。ただ一つ問題なのは、同じ職場にいるので毎日顔を合わせなければならないことです。このようなストレスのある状況はあなたの仕事に影響するかもしれません。

その逆も賢明ではありません。友人や恋人同士がいっしょに働き始めると、しばしば問題が起こります。お金や考えについて喧嘩が始まり、相手に否定的な感情が生まれ、二人の関係にひびが入ることがあります。

28

There are plenty of fish in the sea

proverb

―――※―――

（恋人にふられても）
いい人は、まだたくさんいる

ことわざ

There are plenty of opportunities out there for romance. Don't feel too bad when one relationship ends. There is always a chance for another relationship and hopefully the next one will work out better. You have to keep looking for the right person. Just remember to watch out for sharks.

A I miss Alex so much! I can't stop thinking about him.

B You just need to meet someone new. That will help you get over him.

A But I'll never meet anyone as good as Alex.

B Sure you will. *There are plenty of fish in the sea*. Just get out there and start looking.

・・・

世の中にはロマンスの機会がたくさんあります。二人の関係が終わったからって、そんなに嘆かないでください。必ず新たな出会いの機会があり、運が良ければ、次のほうがうまくいくかもしれません。適切な人を探し続けてください。ただし鮫にはご用心を。

A アレックスに会えなくてとてもさみしいわ！　つい彼のことを考えてしまう。

B 誰か別の人と出会わなきゃだめね。そうすれば、彼のことを忘れられるわ。

A でも、アレックスほどいい人には会えないと思う。

B きっと会えるわ。いい人は、まだたくさんいるもの。外に出て探せばいいのよ。

29

Understanding is a two-way street

Eleanor Roosevelt, *First Lady & activist (1884–1962)*

理解とは双方向なものだ

エレノア・ルーズベルト
ファーストレディー・活動家(1884～1962)

Understanding must go both ways in order to be true understanding.

If you want someone to understand you, then you must try to understand that person, too. If you want someone to listen to you, then you must listen to him or her in return. If you want people to respect your opinions, then you must respect their opinions. This is true even if your opinions are different from theirs.

People have different personalities and opinions, which can be hard to understand. It is easy to think: "how can somebody be like that?" Or: "how can somebody actually think like that?" However, another person might think the same way about you!

Try to understand why somebody thinks or feels a particular way. Hopefully, in return, he or she will do the same for you.

・・・

真に相手を理解するには、双方向に理解しなくてはなりません。

誰かに自分のことを理解してもらいたかったら、あなたもその人のことを理解しようとするべきです。誰かに自分の言うことを聞いてもらいたかったら、お返しにあなたもその人の言うことを聞くべきです。人に自分の意見を尊重してもらいたかったら、あなたも彼らの意見を尊重するべきです。たとえ彼らと意見が違っていてもそうするべきです。

人は様々な性格と意見を持っていますので、それを理解するのが難しいこともあります。つい、「どうしてあんな人がいるんだ？」とか、「どうしてあんなふうに考える人がいるんだ」と考えがちです。けれども、相手もあなたに対して同じように考えているかもしれません。

相手がどうしてそんなふうに考えたり感じたりするのか理解しようとしてください。うまくいけば、お返しに相手も同じことをしてくれるでしょう。

30

It takes two to tango

proverb

**タンゴは一人では踊れない
（責任は両方にある）**

ことわざ

Tango, like most kinds of dance, needs two people. Many other things in life also need two people, like friendship and romance for example.

It also takes two people to fight. When you find yourself in a fight, don't put all the blame on the other person. Both people in a fight are responsible. Think about what you could have done differently to prevent the fight from happening. Think about what you can say to stop the fight from continuing. A fight can only continue if you allow it to continue.

　A　Stop it! I don't want to hear anymore. Why are you always shouting at me?

　B　Hey, *it takes two to tango*. Maybe if you listened to me more, then I wouldn't have to shout.

タンゴは、たいていのダンスと同様に、二人の人が必要です。人生の多くのことにも、例えば友情やロマンスのように、二人の人が必要です。

喧嘩にも二人の人が関わっています。あなたが喧嘩をしているのなら、すべてを相手のせいにしてはなりません。喧嘩は両者に責任があるのです。どんな態度を取っていれば喧嘩を始めずにすんだか考えてください。どう言ったら喧嘩を止められるか考えてください。喧嘩が続くのは、あなたが続けようとする時だけです。

　A　やめろ！　もう何も聞きたくない。どうしていつもぼくに怒鳴りつけるんだ？

　B　ねえ、タンゴは一人では踊れないのよ。たぶん、わたしの言うことをもっと聞いてくれたら、怒鳴る必要なんかなくなるわ。

31

Love is blind

proverb

恋は盲目

ことわざ

Love makes an ordinary person appear wonderful. Love can even make an ordinary person appear perfect. This is because people in love often only see the good side of the person they love. They often don't see the bad. People in love see only what they want to see.

Usually it is a good thing that love is blind. After all, nobody is perfect! If love weren't blind, none of us would be loved at all. On the other hand, love can also be dangerous. Love can make people do things that they wouldn't normally do.

- **A** What does she see in him?
- **B** I have no idea. *Love is blind.*

・・・

恋をすると平凡な人がすてきに見えます。恋をすると平凡な人が完璧に見えることさえあります。なぜなら、恋をした人は恋する相手の良い面しか見ないことが多いからです。悪い面を見ないことが多いのです。恋をした人は見たいものしか見ません。

たいていは、恋は盲目というのは都合の良いことです。結局のところ、完璧な人などいないのですから。恋が盲目でなければ、誰も恋してもらえません。別の見方をすれば、恋は危険でもあります。恋をした人は普通だったらやらないことをするからです。

- **A** 彼女は彼のどこを見ているんだろう？
- **B** わからないねえ。恋は盲目だから。

32

Time heals all wounds

proverb

時はすべての傷を癒やす

ことわざ

With time, even a heart that is broken will heal.

When you feel bad, it is hard to imagine that you will ever feel better. However, with time you will feel better. As time goes by, the pain will become less and less. The deeper the wound, the more time it may take. Just be patient and let time do its work.

Do you remember your first broken heart? Was it last year? Five years ago? Twenty years ago? At the time, it must have hurt a lot. Maybe you thought you would never fall in love again! However, with each passing year it hurts less and less. If it happened a long time ago, maybe it doesn't hurt at all now.

Each time someone breaks your heart, it hurts all over again. Remember that with time, your heart will heal again, just as it did in the past.

・・

時がたてば、壊れた心さえ癒えるでしょう。

つらい時は、気持ちが楽になるなんて想像もできません。けれども、時がたてば気持ちが楽になります。時がたつと痛みはだんだん小さくなります。傷が深いほど時間がかかるかもしれません。ただじっと我慢して、時が癒やしてくれるのを待ちましょう。

初めて失恋したときのことを覚えていますか。それは去年ですか、5年前ですか、それとも20年前ですか。そのころはきっと深く傷ついたでしょう。もしかしたら、もう二度と恋なんかしたくないと思ったかもしれません。けれども、年月がたつにつれて傷は薄れていきます。ずっと昔のことなら、今はまったく痛みがないかもしれません。

誰かがあなたの心を壊すたびに、痛みは繰り返しおそってきます。時がたてば、昔そうであったように、心は再び癒えることを忘れないでください。

33

It is not fair to ask of others what you are unwilling to do yourself

Eleanor Roosevelt, *First Lady & activist (1884–1962)*

あなたがやりたくないことを他人に頼むのは、フェアではありません

エレノア・ルーズベルト
ファーストレディー・活動家(1884〜1962)

If you don't want to do something, then other people probably don't want to do it either. If something is difficult for you to do, it is probably difficult for someone else to do, too.

It is easy to think: "He is stronger than me, so he can do it." Or: "She is more confident than I am, so I'll ask her to do it." However, that person may not be as strong or as confident as he or she appears to be. It might not be as easy as you think for that person to do the thing that you asked.

Think about how you would feel if someone asked you to do the same thing. Would you want to say "no"? Would you be able to say "no"? Asking someone to do something can put that person in a difficult situation. Imagine yourself in the same situation before asking someone to do something.

もしあなたが何かをやりたくないのなら、たぶん、ほかの人だってやりたくないでしょう。もしあなたにとって何かをすることが難しいなら、おそらくほかの人にとっても難しいでしょう。

「彼はぼくより強いから、彼ならできる」とか、「彼女はわたしより自信に満ちているから、彼女に頼もう」などと考えがちです。けれども、その人は見掛けほど強くも、自信に満ちているわけでもないかもしれません。あなたに頼まれたことをすることは、その人にとってはあなたが考えるほど簡単ではないかもしれません。

もしあなたが同じことを頼まれたらどんなふうに感じるか考えてください。「できない」と言いたいのではありませんか。「できない」と言えますか。人に何かを頼むと、その人を苦しい立場に置くことがあります。人に何かを頼む前に、自分が同じ立場だったらどうするか想像してください。

34

Treat others the way you would like to be treated

proverb

自分にしてもらいたいことを人にしてあげなさい

ことわざ

This proverb is called the "golden rule." Children in America usually learn it on their first day of school. It is called the "golden rule," the teacher says, because it is the most important rule in the world.

For children, the message is simple: if you don't want someone to hit you, don't hit other people. If you don't want to be shouted at, don't shout at other people. If you don't want someone to say mean things about you, then don't say mean things about other people.

Adults, on the other hand, seem to have forgotten the message. Too often we make up excuses or blame other people instead of taking responsibility for our actions. Next time you feel yourself about to do something unkind, remind yourself of the "golden rule."

・・

このことわざは「黄金律」と呼ばれています。アメリカの子どもたちは普通、初めて学校に行った日に学びます。先生がこれを「黄金律」と呼ぶのは、世界で一番大切な規則だからです。

子どもたちにとってこのメッセージは簡単です。誰かに叩かれたくないのなら、ほかの人を叩いてはいけない。怒鳴られるのがいやなら、ほかの人を怒鳴らない。自分の悪口を言われたくないのなら、ほかの人の悪口を言わない、ということです。

これに対して、大人たちはこのメッセージを忘れてしまったように見えます。あまりにもひんぱんに言い訳をしたり他者のせいにしたりして、自分の行動の責任を取ろうとしません。今度自分が何か不親切なことをしようとしていると感じたら、この「黄金律」を思い出してください。

35

Let sleeping dogs lie

proverb

寝た子を起こすな

ことわざ

On't cause trouble. Don't argue about something that happened in the past. Leave the past in the past. Don't bring the past into the present where it can cause trouble again. The noisy dogs have finally gone to sleep. Don't wake them up again!

If talking about something will cause more trouble than staying quiet, it is better to stay quiet.

   A I can't believe you got us lost again!

   B We're not lost. We just need to…

   A That's what you said in Rome! Don't you remember? We walked for hours in the rain and then it started to get dark…

   B Why did you have to bring that up now? Can't you just *let sleeping dogs lie*?

わざわざ問題を起こすようなことをしないでください。過去のことで言い争ってはなりません。過去は過去として水に流しましょう。過去のことを現在に持ち出して問題を蒸し返さないでください。騒々しい犬がようやく眠ったのです。再び起こしてはなりません。

何かについて話すことが黙っているより問題を起こすようなら、黙っているのが賢明です。

   A あなたのせいでまた迷ってしまうなんて、信じられない。

   B 迷ったんじゃない。ただ必要なのは……。

   A ローマでもそう言ったじゃない。忘れたの？　雨の中を何時間も歩いてそのうち暗くなってきて……。

   B どうして今そんなことを持ち出すんだ？　「寝た子を起こすな」って言うじゃないか。

36

If you look for the bad in people, you'll surely find it

Abraham Lincoln, *President (1809–1865)*

もし人々の中に「悪」を探すなら、それは確実に見つかるだろう

エイブラハム・リンカーン

大統領(1809〜1865)

Every person has a good side and a bad side. If you look for the good side, you can easily find it. If you look for the bad side, you can easily find that, too.

Your own attitudes and opinions affect how you see other people. Do you think people are generally good or generally bad? How quickly do you make up your mind about someone? If someone acts badly once, do you think he or she is a bad person? If someone acts badly, do you expect that he or she will always act badly?

Often people see what they expect to see. If you expect to see the good, then that is what you will see. If you expect to see the bad, then that is what you will see. Look for the good in people if that is what you want to see.

・・

どの人にも良い面と悪い面があります。人の良い面を探そうとすれば、簡単に見つけられます。悪い面を探しても、簡単に見つけられます。

あなた自身の態度や意見が、あなたが他人を見る目に反映されます。あなたは人は概して良いと思いますか、それとも概して悪いと思いますか。どれくらいの早さで誰かに対する判断をくだしますか。誰かが一度でも悪い行動をすれば、その人を悪い人だと考えますか。誰かが悪い行動をすれば、その人はいつも悪い行動をすると思いますか。

人はしばしば、自分が見たいと思うものを見ようとします。良い面を見たいと思えば、良い面が見えるでしょう。悪い面を見たいと思えば、悪い面が見えるでしょう。人の良い面を見たいなら、それを探してください。

37

Absence makes the heart grow fonder

proverb

遠ざかるほど想いは募る

ことわざ

Spend time away from the person you love, and you will love him or her more.

It can be difficult to spend a lot of time with someone. The more time you spend with someone, the more you will see his or her bad side. There will be little things that he or she says or does that make you angry. After all, nobody is perfect! Sometimes the bad can make us forget about the good.

However, when the person is gone, memories of the good come back. When you miss someone, you remember all the good things about him or her. This is why it is important for couples to spend some time apart.

・・・

好きな人と離れて時を過ごすと、その人のことをもっと好きになります。

誰かと長い時間過ごすのが面倒な時があります。いっしょに過ごす時間が長くなるほど、相手の欠点が目につきます。相手が言ったりしたりするささいなことに腹が立つこともあります。そもそも完璧な人などいないのです。時には、悪い面ばかり目について良い面を忘れてしまうことだってあります。

けれども、その人がいなくなると、良いことばかり思い出されます。誰かのことが恋しくなると、その人のすべての良い面を思い出します。このため、恋人や夫婦がしばらく離れて時を過ごすことが大切なのです。

38

If you can't say anything nice, don't say anything at all

proverb

もし良いことが言えないのであれば、何も言うな

ことわざ

If you have to choose between saying something unkind and saying nothing, say nothing. If saying something nice would be a lie, then say nothing instead.

Parents teach their children this because they want their children to be polite. However, this proverb is sometimes used to be anything but polite! It can be used to give an honest opinion indirectly. For example, two friends might have a conversation like this:

A What do you think of my new hairstyle?

B Hmm… My mom always told me that *if you can't say anything nice, don't say anything at all*.

So what the person is really saying is: "I can't say anything about your hairstyle because I can't say anything nice about it—because I don't like it at all."

・・・

不親切なことを言うか何も言わないかどちらか選べと言われたら、何も言わないでください。何か良いことを言おうとしてもそれが嘘なら、むしろ何も言わないでください。

親が子どもにこれを教えるのは、子どもに礼儀正しくなって欲しいからです。けれどもこのことわざは、礼儀正しくさせたい時以外にも用いることがあります。正直な意見を遠回しに言う時に用いることができます。例えば、二人の友人がこんな会話をするかもしれません。

A わたしの新しいヘアースタイルどう思う？

B うーん……。「もし良いことが言えないのであれば、何も言うな」っていつもママが言うんだ。

ここでBが本当に言いたかったのは、「きみのヘアースタイルについて何も言えないよ。だって、何も良いことを言えないから。つまり、まったく気に入らないからさ」ということなのです。

39

Two's company, three's a crowd

proverb

二人は仲間、三人は人込み

ことわざ

Whhen it comes to romance or close friends, two is the natural number. A third person can feel strange or out of place. When two people seem to like each other, it is best to leave them alone. You don't want to get in the way of a romance.

A What are you doing tonight?
B Oh, Lisa and I are going to go to the movies.
A I haven't seen a movie in a long time. Mind if I join you?
B Sorry. I'm afraid *three's a crowd*.
A Oh, I see! I hope you two have a good time.

ロマンスや親友に関しては、二人が自然な数です。三人目の人は落ち着かない気持ちや場違いな気持ちになることがあります。二人が好意を寄せ合っているように見えるなら、そっとしておくのが最善です。ロマンスの邪魔などしたくありませんからね。

A 今夜どうするの？
B ああ、リサと映画を観に行く予定だ。
A ぼくは長いあいだ、映画を観ていないんだ。いっしょに行ってもいいかな？
B 悪いけど遠慮してくれ。「三人は人込み」って言うから。
A ああ、そうだったね。二人で楽しんでくれ。

40

Misery loves company

proverb

同病相憐れむ

ことわざ

People who are unhappy look for other people who are unhappy.

Someone who has problems often wants to talk about his or her problems. Someone in a difficult situation may want to complain about it. However, that person needs a listener—someone to listen to the talking and complaining. The best listener is another unhappy person. When two unhappy people get together, they can complain about their problems to each other.

Sometimes you have an unhappy friend who wants to talk to you about his or her problems. Maybe he or she wants advice. Of course you should support your friend. However, be careful that his or her unhappy feelings don't spread to you. When one person starts complaining, it is easy for another to start complaining, too.

不幸せな人は、別の不幸せな人を探します。

問題を抱えている人は、しばしば自分の問題について話したがります。困難な状況にいる人は、それについて不平を言いたくなるかもしれません。けれども、それには聞き手が必要です。つまり、話や不平を聞いてくれる人のことです。最良の聞き手は、別の不幸せな人です。不幸せな人が二人集まると、自分たちの問題について不平を言い合うことができます。

時には、自分の問題をあなたに話したがる不幸せな友人ができることがあります。おそらく友人は助言が欲しいのかもしれません。もちろん、あなたはその友人を支えるべきです。けれども、その人の不幸せな感情があなたに移らないように気をつけてください。人が不平を言い始めたら、もう一人もつい不平を言ってしまいますから。

41

Knowledge speaks, but wisdom listens

Jimi Hendrix, *musician (1942–1970)*

知識はものを言う。だが知恵は耳を傾ける

ジミ・ヘンドリックス
ミュージシャン(1942〜1970)

Smart people speak; even smarter people listen. Through speaking, you can share what you know with other people. Through listening, you can learn from others. Only through listening can you get new knowledge, so listening can actually make you smarter.

Everybody knows how much Americans love to talk. Often in America it seems like everyone just wants to be heard and no one wants to listen. That's why advice like this is necessary. It reminds us that sometimes the best thing you can do in a situation is to keep your mouth closed. Of course not everyone wants to listen to this advice!

・・・

賢い人は話し、もっと賢い人は耳を傾けます。話をすることで、自分の知っていることをほかの人たちと共有できます。耳を傾けることで、ほかの人たちから学べます。耳を傾けることを通してのみ、新しい知識を得られます。ですから耳を傾けるともっと賢くなれるのです。

アメリカ人がどれほど話好きか誰もが知っています。アメリカでは、聞いてもらいたい人ばかりで聞きたい人がいないことが多くあるようです。だから、このような助言が必要なのです。この助言は、時にはある状況で自分にできる最善のことは口を閉じておくことだと気づかせてくれます。だからと言って、誰もがこの助言を聞きたいわけではないでしょう！

42

Good fences make good neighbors

proverb

親しき仲にも礼儀あり

ことわざ

A fence marks the line in between two houses. A good, strong fence will keep noise, dogs, and baseballs on the side where they belong. It will stop the children next door from picking apples from the neighbor's tree. Having a fence means that two families can live side by side and still have their own space. The less neighbors fight over little things—like whose dog went into whose garden—the more they like each other.

Fences draw a clear line between what belongs to one person and what belongs to another. The clearer these lines are, the less there is to argue about. This is true not just among neighbors but also among friends and co-workers.

垣根は隣り合った家の境界線になります。良くできたしっかりした垣根があれば、騒音をさえぎり、犬や野球ボールがこちらにくることもありません。近所の子どもたちが隣家の木のリンゴを取るのを防いでくれます。垣根があるということは、二家族が隣同士に住みながら、なお自分自身の場所を持てるということです。隣人と、どこそこの犬がどこそこの庭に入ったというような、ささいなことでもめることが少なくなるほど、お互いに仲良くできます。

垣根はある人の所有物と別の人の所有物のあいだに明確な境界線を引いてくれます。この線が明確なほど、口論が少なくなります。このことは隣人同士だけではく、友人や仕事仲間に対しても言えます。

43

Good friends are hard to find

proverb

良い友達は見つけるのが難しい

ことわざ

The difference between a friend and a good friend is huge. A friend is someone who comes to your birthday party when you invite him or her. A good friend is someone who always remembers your birthday without having to be told. A friend is someone whom you can meet for coffee and talk about many things. A good friend is someone with whom you can talk about everything. A good friend is someone who will be there for you no matter what happens.

Good friends are a lot harder to find than ordinary friends. When times are difficult, it is easy to understand who your good friends really are. They are the ones who offer their support. Count yourself lucky to have these people in your life—they are rare.

友人と良い友人のあいだには大きな差があります。友人とはあなたが招待したときに誕生パーティにきてくれる人です。良い友人とは言われなくてもいつもあなたの誕生日を覚えていてくれる人です。友人とはいっしょにコーヒーを飲んだりたくさんのことをおしゃべりしたりする人です。良い友人とは何もかも話すことができる人です。良い友人とは何が起ころうともそこにいてくれる人のことです。

良い友人を見つけることは普通の友人を見つけるよりずっと難しいものです。困難な時期には、誰が本当に良い友人かすぐにわかります。支援してくれるのが良い友人です。生涯にそのような人を得られたことを幸運だと思ってください。そんな人はめったに見つからないのですから。

Love and Friendships

"Don't judge a book by its cover" may lose its usefulness as people come to read more material on tablets and other digital devices, but that doesn't mean the fundamental idea will change. Alternatives can include "What really matters is not obvious to the naked eye" or "Look beneath the surface."

The reverse of this proverb is the uncommon "WYSIWYG", an acronym for "What you see is what you get," which is used with computers. It means that what you see on the monitor is what will be printed on paper. But "What you see is what you get" is also used as good advice. It means that if you look carefully at the surface of something, you can probably guess its true inner nature. Just because a guy looks like a tough guy doesn't necessarily mean that he is one, but, on the other hand, his appearance may say something about what is in his heart.

The comment that "Love is blind" seems quite outdated, but the wisdom of the proverb can be restated as "I don't

愛と友情

> 進化する
> 「ことわざ」を
> 使いこなす！

「本の中身を装丁で判断するな」とは、人々がタブレットや他の電子機器で文章を読むようになった時代に、もはや有用性を逸した感がありますが、その根本的な考えに変わりはありません。言い換えるならば、「本当に重要なことは肉眼では見えない」あるいは「物事の内面を見なさい」といったものになるでしょう。

このことわざの反対表現は、あまり見慣れない "WYSIWYG" で表すことができます。これは「目に見えるものは得ることができる」というコンピュータ関連の言い回しの頭字語です。つまり、パソコンの画面に表示された内容が、そのまま紙に印刷できる、ということを意味しています。しかし、「目に見えるものは得ることができる」という表現は、いいアドバイスとしても使えます。すなわち、何かの表面を注意深く見ていると、おそらく、その内側にある本質がわかってくるだろう、ということなのです。強い男に見えるからといって、必ずしも強いわけではありませんが、一方、姿形はその内面を表すとも言えるのです。

「恋は盲目」という言い方はとても古臭い感がありますが、ことわざ的に言い換えるならば、「彼が彼女の本性をわかっているのかわからない」あるいは「誰にでも自分の好みを言う権利はある」など

know what he sees in her" or "To each her [his] own." We might go a step further and comment, "She must be Superwoman. Maybe she can see something in him that we can't." In other words, the wisdom of the proverb is still there, but it is updated a bit.

The true nature of friendship—and love as well—is expressed in "Treat others the way you would like to be treated," which is found in the Christian prayer "Do unto others as you would have them do unto you." "If you can't say anything nice, don't say anything at all" is similar advice which takes the other person's feelings into account. There are two sides to "If you look for the bad in people, you will surely find it." The straightforward interpretation of this is that everyone has bad points. The reverse of this is implied: If you look for the good in people, you will surely find it.

進化する「ことわざ」を使いこなす！

でしょうか。さらに一段上がって、「彼女はスーパーウーマンに違いない。たぶん彼女には、誰にも見ることができない彼の本性が見えるんだよ」と言うこともできるでしょう。つまり、ことわざの英知というものは常に存在し、少しずつ更新されているのです。

　友情の本質というものは——愛についても言えることですが——「自分にしてもらいたいことを人にしてあげなさい」と表現することができます。この表現は「己の欲するところ人にもこれを施せ」というように聖書にも記されています。「いいことを言えないのなら、何も言うな」というのも似たようなアドバイスで、他人の心情を 慮 っています。「他人の短所を探せば、必ず見つけることができるだろう」という表現には二面性があります。直接的な言い換えとしては、誰にでも悪いところはある、ということ。裏を返せば、他人の長所を探せば、必ず見つけることができるだろう、ということが暗示されているのです。

Human Nature
人間の本性

44

The grass is always greener on the other side of the fence

proverb

隣の庭の芝生はいつも青い

ことわざ

Your neighbor has a nicer car than you. Your best friend often travels to foreign countries for work. If only you could have a nicer car. If only you could travel to foreign countries more often. Then, maybe you would be happier.

On the other hand, your neighbor hates his car because it uses too much gas. He wishes that he had your car. Maybe your friend is tired of traveling. She wants to spend more time at home.

What you don't have often looks better than what you do have. That doesn't mean it is better. Stop wishing for something else and be happy with what you have. Also, stop looking over the neighbor's fence.

隣人があなたよりいい車を持っています。親友は仕事でひんぱんに海外に行きます。いい車を持つことさえできれば、もっとひんぱんに海外旅行ができさえすれば、たぶんあなたはもっと幸せになれるのでしょう。

その一方で、あなたの隣人はガソリンを食いすぎる自分の車を好きになれません。彼はあなたの車ならいいのにと思っています。たぶん、あなたの友人は旅行に疲れているかもしれません。彼女はもっと家で過ごしたいと望んでいます。

自分の持っていないものが持っているものより良く見えることが多くあります。そうかといって、持っていないもののほうがいいわけではありません。ほかのものを欲しがるのをやめ、持っているもので満足してください。それから、垣根越しに隣をのぞいてはなりません。

45

Hindsight is always 20-20

Billy Wilder, *filmmaker (1906–2002)*

あと知恵はいつも完璧

ビリー・ワイルダー
映画製作者（1906～2002）

Hindsight is the view of the past from the position of the present. 20-20 vision is perfect vision. It is much easier to understand clearly what happened in the past than to see clearly what is happening in the present.

After a relationship has finished, it is easy to understand what you did right and what you did wrong. You can see which decisions changed your relationship for the better or for the worse. You can look back and realize what was really important and what wasn't. It is hard to see this from the present, particularly because you don't know what will happen in the future.

Often people make mistakes that they don't realize. Sometimes they fail to understand what their partner wants or needs. Only later do they understand what they should have done. The only problem is that it is often too late.

・・

あと知恵とは現在の位置から過去を眺めることです。20–20とは正常な視力のことです。過去に起こったことを明確に理解するほうが現在起こっていることを明確に理解するより、はるかに簡単です。

人との関係が終わったあとは、自分がしたことの何が正しかったのか何が間違っていたのか簡単に理解できます。どの決定が両者の関係を良いほうにそれとも悪いほうに変えたか見えてきます。振り返って、何が本当に大切で何がそうでなかったか理解できます。現在の位置から現在のことを見る場合、このようなことを理解するのは難しくなります。特に、将来、何が起こるかわからないからです。

人は間違いを犯してもそれに気づかないことがよくあります。時には、自分のパートナーが何を望んで何を必要としているかわからないこともあります。あとになってはじめて、どうすべきだったかわかるのです。ただ一つの問題は、たいてい遅すぎるということです。

# 46

Nobody is perfect

proverb

完璧な人間などいない

ことわざ

Everybody makes mistakes. No matter how hard you try to be perfect, it is only natural that you will make mistakes sometimes. Even though you make mistakes, you still hope to be loved and forgiven, right? In return, try to love and forgive others even when they make mistakes.

Don't expect someone to be perfect, no matter how badly you want him or her to be! When it comes to relationships between people, you cannot take the good without some of the bad.

   A I've been waiting for half an hour!
   B I'm sorry. Work finished late. I got here as fast as I could.
   A You could have called.
   B I already said I was sorry. Come on, *nobody's perfect*. Are you going to stay mad at me all night?
   A Maybe.

誰だって間違いを犯します。どんなに完璧であろうとしても、時には間違うのはまったく自然なことです。あなたはたとえ間違いを犯しても、やはり愛されて許されたいと思うのではありませんか。その代わり、ほかの人が間違いを犯しても、その人を愛して許そうとしてください。

人に完璧を望んではなりません。どれほどそうあって欲しいと望んでも、そうしてはなりません。人間関係において、少しばかりの悪い点を受け入れずに良い点だけを求めることはできません。

   A もう30分も待ったのよ。
   B 悪かった。遅くまで仕事があったんだ。大急ぎできたんだよ。
   A 電話してくれればよかったのに。
   B 悪いとあやまっているだろう。なあ、完璧な人間などいないんだよ。一晩中怒っているつもりかい？
   A たぶんね。

119

47

Old habits die hard

proverb

身についた習慣はなかなか変わらない

ことわざ

Habits, especially bad habits, are hard to break. The older the habit is, the harder it is to break.

Even though it might be hard to break a habit, people still try. At least people often say they are going to try. That doesn't mean that they will actually succeed. Will someone who has smoked for 40 years really be able to quit? Of course, people can change and sometimes they do. We should be happy and surprised if they do; however, we shouldn't expect people to change just because they say they are going to change.

- **A** I ran into Joe last weekend at a bar.
- **B** What? I thought he had given up drinking.
- **A** You know what they say, *old habits die hard*.

習慣、特に悪い習慣をやめることは難しいです。昔からの習慣ほどやめるのが難しくなります。

習慣をやめるのは困難かもしれませんが、それでも人は試します。少なくとも、やってみるつもりだと言うことはよくあります。だからと言って、実際に成功するわけではありません。40年も喫煙してきた人が、本当に禁煙できるでしょうか。もちろん、人は変わりますし、時には成功することもあります。そんなことが起これば、喜んで、驚いてあげればいいでしょう。でも、人が自分を変えると宣言したからといって変わると期待するべきではありません。

- **A** この前の週末、バーでばったりジョーに会ったよ。
- **B** 何だって？ あいつはアルコールをやめたと思ったけれど。
- **A** よく言うじゃないか。「身についた習慣はなかなか変わらない」って。

121

48

Nice guys finish last

Leo Durocher, *baseball manager (1906–1991)*

お人好しでは勝てない

レオ・ドローチャー

野球監督(1906〜1991)

Actually Leo Durocher didn't say these exact words. He said that a team had nice players, but that they were in last place. A clever newspaper editor changed his original sentence into this famous headline. Even though the words weren't correct, they quickly became popular. Such is the power of the media!

But is it true? Do nice guys really finish last? It often seems that in work and in relationships, nice guys can't win. In business, being nice can make you look weak. In relationships, women say they want a nice guy but often choose a bad one instead.

If it is true, however, it is because we make it true. If you don't want the nice guys to finish last, give them more respect. Make sure they don't always finish last!

レオ・ドローチャーがこの通りに言ったわけではありません。実際は、チームにすばらしい選手がいたのに最下位に終わったと言いました。頭の切れる新聞編集者が元の言葉をこの有名な見出しに変えたのです。言葉通りでなくても、すぐに評判になりました。これこそマスコミの力ですね。

でもこれは本当でしょうか。お人好しは本当に最下位になるのでしょうか。仕事や恋愛関係で、お人好しが勝てないことがよくあるように感じられます。ビジネスの世界では、お人好しだと弱く見られます。恋愛関係では、女性は善良な人が好きだと言いながら、ちょっとワルを選ぶことがよくあります。

けれども、これが本当なら、わたしたちのせいです。いい人に損をして欲しくないなら、彼らにもっと敬意を払うべきです。そうすることで、いい人ばかりが常に最下位にならないようにしましょう。

49

Beauty is only skin deep

proverb

美人も皮一重

ことわざ

Beauty is only what you see on the surface. A beautiful outside does not mean a beautiful inside. Someone may be attractive, but he or she also may be unkind. On the other hand, someone who isn't attractive may be a wonderful person! It's the whole person that counts—and the skin is only a small part of the whole person. The more time you spend with someone, the more this becomes true.

A Have you met Joe's new girlfriend? She's really beautiful.

B Yeah. But have you spent any time with her? She's so boring—no personality at all. If I were him, I wouldn't be able to stand it.

A Really? That's too bad. I guess it's true what people say about *beauty being only skin deep*.

....

美人というのは単に表面上のことです。外見が美しいからと言って、内面が美しいというわけではありません。魅力的な人がいても、その人は不親切かもしれません。これに反して、外見は魅力的でなくてもすばらしい人がいるかもしれません。大事なのはその人全体です。外見はその人全体のほんの一部なのです。誰かと長い時間を過ごすほど、これが真実だということがわかります。

A ジョーの新しい彼女を見たかい？　すごい美人だよ。

B そうかい。でも、彼女と少しでもいっしょにいたことがあるかい？　すごく退屈だよ。まったく個性がないんだ。ぼくがジョーなら、とても我慢できないよ。

A 本当？　それはひどいね。「美人も皮一重」というのは本当のようだね。

125

50

Man cannot live on bread alone

proverb

人はパンだけで生きるものではない

ことわざ

Men—and women, too!—need basic things to survive. We need air to breathe, water to drink, food to eat, and a house to protect us from the sun and rain. However, a life with only these basic things would be a sad and lonely one. People also need family and friends; we need music and laughter.

Work is important, but it is not the only important thing in life. Make sure to make time for the other important things. As the actress Marilyn Monroe once famously said: "A career is wonderful, but you can't curl up with it on a cold night."

男の人も女の人も、生きるためには基本的なものが必要です。息をする空気、飲み水、食料、それに日射しや雨から身を守ってくれる家がいります。けれども、このような基本的なものだけの人生は悲しくて寂しいものです。人には家族や友人が必要です。音楽や笑いだって必要です。

仕事は大切ですが、人生で大切なものはそれだけではありません。必ず、ほかの大切なことのための時間をつくるようにしてください。女優のマリリン・モンローが言った有名な言葉のように、「仕事はすばらしいけれど、寒い夜に仕事を抱えて丸くなるわけにはいかない」のです。

51

A person's a person no matter how small

Dr. Seuss, *author (1904–1991)*

どんなに小さくても人は人

ドクター・スース
作家(1904〜1991)

This line is from a famous children's book. The main point of the book is this: even small people have something to say. Their voices might be small, but that means we should try extra hard to hear them. What's more, many small people can come together to make one big voice. Then they can be noisy.

But what does it mean to be a "small person"? In this case, small doesn't mean short. It means someone who is often ignored. It could be someone who is so poor or so young that people don't listen seriously to what he or she says. However these "small people" are people, too! We should give them the same respect that we give the "big people."

・・・

これは有名な絵本のせりふです。本の主題は、小さな人でも言いたいことがあるということです。彼らの声は小さいかもしれませんが、そのぶん彼らの声を一生懸命に聞こうと努めるべきです。さらに、小さな人がたくさん集まれば一つの大きな声になります。そうなったら、騒々しくなるかもしれません。

ところで、「小さな人」には、どんな意味があるのでしょう。ここでは、小さいというのは背が低いということではありません。しょっちゅう無視される人のことです。とても貧しかったり幼かったりして、自分の言うことを真剣に聞いてもらえない人のことです。それでも、このような「小さな人たち」も人間なのです！「大きな人たち」に対するときと同じ敬意を彼らにも払わなくてはなりません。

52

The apple doesn't fall far from the tree

proverb

蛙の子は蛙
（リンゴは木からあまり遠いところへは落ちない）

ことわざ

It is not surprising that children follow what their parents do. Just as apples come from trees, children come from their parents. They will have many things in common, even after the children grow up and move away. The seeds from the apple will grow into new trees, and the pattern will continue.

This isn't the only proverb that compares people to apples. Another one is "one bad apple spoils the whole bunch." This means that one bad person in the group can make the whole group look bad.

- **A** Did your daughter decide what she wants to study?
- **B** She's going to study science like her dad.
- **A** *The apple doesn't fall far from the tree*, does it?
- **B** Not in her case! My son, on the other hand…

．．

子どもが親のすることを見習うのは驚くことではありません。リンゴが木に実るように、子どもは親から生まれるのですから。親子には共通点がたくさんあります。たとえ子どもが成長し家を出ても、それは変わりません。リンゴの種は育って新しい木になり、それが繰り返されます。

人をリンゴに例えたことわざはほかにもあります。もう一つは、「腐ったリンゴは周りのものを駄目にする」です。集団のなかに悪い人が一人いると、集団全体が悪く思われるという意味です。

- **A** お嬢さんは何を勉強するか決めましたか。
- **B** 父親と同じように科学を勉強するようです。
- **A** 「リンゴは木からあまり遠いところへは落ちない」ということですね。
- **B** 娘の場合はそうです。一方で息子は……。

131

53

Hunger is the best sauce

proverb

空腹は最上のソース

ことわざ

Nothing tastes as good as it does when you're hungry. Even the most ordinary food will taste extraordinary to someone who really needs it. On the other hand, to someone who is not hungry, the same food won't taste as good. It might even taste bad! Desire has a taste of its own. Cooks may spend years studying how to make perfect sauces; however, hunger is the one ingredient they can't control.

A I think this is the best hamburger I've ever eaten.

B You're just saying that because we've been walking for hours and haven't eaten anything all day.

A Maybe so. In that case, *hunger is the best sauce*.

空腹な時ほど食べものがおいしく感じられることはありません。ごく普通の食べものでさえ、それを必要とする人にとってはすばらしいご馳走になります。これに対して、空腹でない人にとっては同じ食べものもそれほどおいしく感じられません。まずく感じることさえあります。食欲にはそれ自体に味があるのでしょう。料理人は何年も研究を重ね最高のソースをつくろうとしているかもしれません。けれども空腹だけはどうすることもできない材料なのです。

A こんなうまいハンバーガーを食べたことがないよ。

B きみがそう言うのは、何時間も歩いて、一日中、何も食べていないからだよ。

A おそらくね。そんな時、空腹は最上のソースだからね。

54

Most people are about as happy as they make their minds up to be

Abraham Lincoln, *President (1809–1865)*

多くの人は自分が幸福になろうと決心した程度だけ幸福である

エイブラハム・リンカーン

大統領(1809〜1865)

It is often said that "happiness is a state of mind." By simply choosing to be happy, you can actually become happy.

Do you usually see the bad side of a situation? Do you get angry or sad over small things? If you answered "yes" to either question, you might not be as happy as you could be. The good news is that you can change. Choose to see the good in a situation instead of the negative. Choose to forgive and forget small things instead of getting angry. By making these small changes, you can choose to be happier.

There are a lot of things beyond your control. Don't give up control over the one important thing you can control—your attitude.

・・・

「幸せは心の持ち方」だとよく言われます。ただ幸せになろうと決心するだけで、本当に幸せになれるのです。

あなたはいつも物事の悪い面を見ますか？ 小さなことに腹を立てたり悲しんだりしますか？ どちらかの質問に「はい」と答えた人は、本来あるべき姿ほど幸せではないかもしれません。幸いにも、あなたは変わることができます。物事の悪い面を見るのではなく良い面を見るようにしてください。小さなことに腹を立てるより許して忘れるようにしてください。このような小さな変化を重ねることで、あなたはもっと幸せになれます。

自分ではどうすることもできないことは山ほどあります。自分の思い通りにできる一つの大切なものを制することを、あきらめないでください。それはあなたの心の持ちようです。

55

One man's trash is another man's treasure

proverb

捨てる神あれば拾う神あり

ことわざ

Things have different value for different people. This is because different people have different needs. One person puts an old piece of furniture out on the street because he doesn't need it. To him, it's trash. Another person, who does need it, picks it up and takes it home. To him, it's treasure. Just because you don't want something doesn't mean that nobody wants it.

A What's in all these bags?

B Oh, just some old clothes that I never wear. I'm going to throw them out.

A Can I have a look? I could use some new clothes for work.

B Sure. But everything in there is really old.

A *One man's trash is another man's treasure*! Hey, this shirt is nice. Can I have it?

B Take anything you want.

・・・

ものの価値は人によって様々です。なぜなら人によって必要なものが違うからです。ある人が古い家具を道端に捨てるのは、もう必要でないからです。その人にとっては、ごみなのです。別の人がそれを必要として、拾って家に持ち帰ります。その人にとっては、宝物です。自分が何かを欲しくないからといって、誰もがそうだというわけではないのです。

A こんなにたくさんの袋に何が入っているの？
B あら、もう着なくなった古い服ばかりよ。捨てようと思っているの。
A 見てもいいかしら。新しい服なら仕事に使えるわ。
B そうね。でもどれも本当に古いのよ。
A 捨てる神あれば拾う神ありよ。あら、すてきなシャツじゃない。もらってもいいかしら？
B 好きなのを持っていって。

137

56

You are as old as you think you are

Muhammad Ali, *athlete (1942–)*

自分の信じた年齢が、自分の年齢となる

モハメド・アリ
運動選手(1942〜)

How old are you? How old do you feel? Age is just a number. It is the number of years that you have been alive. How old you feel depends on your own attitude and experience.

Someone who has had many life experiences may feel older than people who are the same age. Someone who has less experience may feel younger. On the other hand, someone who has a lot of energy will also feel younger, even if he or she is in fact quite old. What's more, the same person can feel either young or old, depending on his or her mood.

How old you feel also depends on what you think it means to be "old." Maybe when you were ten years old, you thought twenty was "old." However, once you become twenty or forty, it doesn't feel as old as you thought it would.

あなたは何歳ですか。何歳のように感じますか。年齢は数字に過ぎません。これまで生きてきた年の数です。何歳に感じるかはあなた自身の態度や経験によって決まります。

人生経験の豊かな人は同年齢の人より年をとった気がするかもしれません。経験の少ない人はもっと若い気がするかもしれません。また一方で、活力にあふれている人は、実際はかなり年をとっていても、若い気がするでしょう。さらに、同じ人でも気分によって若い気がしたり年をとった気がしたりすることがあります。

何歳に感じるかは、「年をとる」という意味のとらえ方によっても決まります。あなたが10歳だったころ、20歳は年をとっていると思ったでしょう。ところが、20歳や40歳になると、思っていたほど年をとっていないと感じるものなのです。

Human Nature

The old proverb "A rolling stone gathers no moss" means different things to different people.

Originally, the proverb saw the growth of "moss" as a desirable trait. It meant that someone who settled in one place could accumulate positive attributes like culture, experience, knowledge and skills. Only by staying in one place, in one situation, or in one place and taking responsibility could one develop the important characteristics of human beings. If one was constantly in motion, jumping from place to place or job to job, that person would end up producing nothing of significance.

In the newer interpretation, "moss" is symbolic of stagnation and lack of ingenuity. In this understanding of the proverb, remaining mobile and agile and trying new things prevent a person from getting "rusty" or "bogged down." This constant motion keeps people sharp and open to new potentials. That's the meaning that the rock group intended when they named themselves The Rolling Stones.

人間の本性

進化する「ことわざ」を使いこなす!

「転石苔むさず」という古いことわざは、人によって異なる内容を意味します。

元来、このことわざは「苔」の成長を望ましい特質であるとみなしていました。ある場所に誰かが定住するようになると、文化、経験、知識、技術といった有用な付加価値が加算されていく、ということを意味していたのです。ある状況下で一カ所に止まってさえいれば、あるいは、一カ所にとどまり責任を取りさえすれば、人間の重要な性質を育むことができるものなのです。居場所を飛び移ったり、職を転々とするなど、常に動きつづけている人は、意義のあるものを生み出すことなく終わってしまうものなのです。

最新の解釈では、「苔」は停滞や創意工夫の欠如の象徴となっています。このことわざをこのように理解すると、機敏に行動し、新しい物事に挑戦することによって、人は錆び付いたり、泥沼に落ち込むことを防ぐことができるというように取ることができます。このように継続的に動きつづけることによって、感覚を研ぎ澄まし、新たな可能性にこころを開くことができるのです。The Rolling Stonesと自らを名付けたロックグループが意図したのは、まさにこういうことなのです。

While it is helpful to understand proverbs like "You are as old as you think you are" or "Kill two birds with one stone" in English, it is not wise to overuse such proverbs in everyday conversation. They are, by nature, cliches, and it is best to use them only when there is no better way to convey your meaning.

We might not agree that "You can't teach an old dog new tricks," but most of us would agree with is "Old habits die hard." We can see this in others and also in ourselves.

Some native speakers of English purposely change these proverbs, so "Everybody's perfect" becomes a parody of "Nobody's perfect." "Nice guys finish last" seems a bit too aggressive, so someone might change it to "Nice guys finish with friends." These are more creative uses of proverbs, but they still depend upon everyone knowing what the original proverb was!

進化する「ことわざ」を使いこなす！

英語で「自分で歳をとっていると思うだけ、歳をとっているものだ」とか「一石二鳥」のようなことわざを理解することは役に立ちますが、このようなことわざを日常会話に使いすぎるのは賢明ではありません。それらは本来使い古された言い回しであり、自分が言いたいことを表現するのに他にふさわしい言い方がないときにのみ使うのがベストでしょう。

「年老いた犬に新しい芸を仕込むことはできない」という表現には同意できませんが、「古い習慣はなかなか改まらない」であれば、ほとんどの人が同意するでしょう。こういったことは、他人にも、我々自身にも、見受けられることなのです。

英語を母国語とする人の中には、わざと、ことわざを言い換えたりすることがあります。たとえば、「誰もが完璧である」は「誰にも過ちはある」のパロディーです。「正直者はバカを見る」は少し言い過ぎですが、これを「正直者はゴールに入るとき、まだ友だちがいる」と言い換える人がいるかもしれません。これらは、さらに創意工夫に富んだ使い方ですが、いずれにせよ、本来の意味を誰もが知っていることが眼目です。

Good Advice

良き助言

57

Don't count your chickens before they've hatched

proverb

―――

捕らぬ狸の皮算用
（卵がかえる前にニワトリの数を数えても意味がない）

ことわざ

You've got eggs, but that doesn't mean that they'll turn into chickens. Success is never certain until it actually happens. Wait until you know for sure, then start counting and making plans.

A How did your presentation go?

B Great. My boss was very happy with it.

A Hey, that's great to hear!

B I'm thinking that, if all goes well, I should finally be able to get that promotion. I can picture it already: a corner office, my name on the door…

A Be careful. *Don't count your chickens before they've hatched*.

B Yeah, I know. But I can dream, can't I?

・・

卵があるからといって、それがニワトリになるというわけではありません。実際に実現しないうちは確実に成功したとは言えません。確実だとわかるまで待って、それから数を数え、計画を立ててください。

A プレゼンテーションの出来はどうだった？

B うまくいったよ。ボスがすごく喜んでくれたよ。

A へえ、すごいじゃないか。

B 考えているんだけれど、すべてうまくいったら、ついに昇進できるんじゃないかって。その姿が目に浮かぶようだ。役員室、ドアの上にはぼくの名前が……。

A 気をつけろよ。卵がかえる前にニワトリの数を数えても意味がない。

B そうだな。だけど夢ぐらい見てもかまわないだろ？

147

58

If you don't like the heat, get out of the kitchen

proverb

仕事の苦しさに耐えられないなら、
仕事を変えよ

ことわざ

Kitchens get hot. If you work in one, you are going to sweat. If you don't like to sweat, then you shouldn't work in a kitchen.

This isn't just about being a cook, though. Any high-pressure job is going to make you sweat. There will be stress, responsibility, and competition. If you can't handle these pressures, then maybe you should work in a job that doesn't have them.

Of course many of the most attractive jobs come with a lot of stress. Before choosing a career, think long and hard about what job best matches your personality and abilities. If you do choose a high-pressure job, don't complain about it—after all, it was your choice. If the stress becomes too much for you, maybe you should look for a different job.

・・

厨房は暑くなります。そのなかで働くと汗をかきます。汗をかきたくないのなら、厨房で働くべきではありません。

ただし、これは料理人に限ったことではありません。プレッシャーが強い仕事はどんな仕事であっても、汗をかきます。ストレス、責任、競争がつきものです。このようなプレッシャーに対処できないのなら、プレッシャーのない仕事をしたほうが良いかもしれません。

もちろん、最も魅力的な仕事には多くのストレスがつきものです。仕事を選ぶ前に、どんな仕事が自分の性格や能力に合っているか、時間をかけてしっかりと考えてください。プレッシャーの強い仕事を選んだのなら、仕事の文句を言ってはなりません。そもそも、あなたが選択したのですから。それでもストレスに耐えられなくなったら、別の仕事を探したほうがいいかもしれません。

59

Don't bite off more than you can chew

proverb

自分の能力以上のことをやろうとするな

ことわざ

Don't try to do too much at once. Be realistic about what you can and cannot do. Don't accept a task if you don't have the skills for it. Don't accept a role if you don't have the time for it—even if that role is very attractive! Think about the other responsibilities you already have. It is better to finish one thing before moving on to the next.

If you attempt to do too much, then maybe you won't be able to complete anything. If you agree to do something that is too difficult for you, you may not be able to do a good job. It is important to have a clear understanding of your abilities and to make realistic decisions.

一度にあまりに多くのことをしようとしてはなりません。できることとできないことを現実的に判断してください。その仕事をする力量がないのなら、引き受けてはなりません。その役目を果たす時間をつくることができないのなら、それがどんなに魅力的であっても、引き受けてはなりません。すでにあなたにかかっているほかの責任について考えてください。一つのことを終えてから、次のことを始めるのが賢明です。

あまりに多くのことをしようとすると、何もやりとげることができないかもしれません。あなたの手にあまることを引き受けた場合、良い仕事ができないかもしれません。大切なのは、自分の能力を明確に理解し、現実的な決定をすることです。

60

Money doesn't grow on trees

proverb

金のなる木はない

ことわざ

Be careful with your money. It is not easily replaced.

If only there were such a thing as a money tree! You could plant it in your garden and have a steady supply of money. Unfortunately, there is no such thing. Money doesn't come that easily to most people. Most people have to work for it. Also, the jobs and family members that provide us with money may not always be around. It is important to keep this in mind when you spend money.

A Hey mom, can I have $50?

B I just gave you $50 yesterday. What happened to that money?

A I spent it already.

B You spend money too quickly. *It doesn't grow on trees*, you know.

・・

お金を無駄づかいしてはなりません。簡単に補うことができないからです。

金のなる木があればいいのに！　庭に植えておけば安定してお金が手に入ります。残念ながら、そんなものはありません。たいていの人にとって、お金はそう容易に手に入れられるものではありません。たいていの人はお金のために働かなくてはなりません。さらに、お金を稼げる仕事や養ってくれる家族が、必ずしも存在するわけではありません。大切なのは、このことを心に刻んでお金を使うことです。

A ねえママ、50ドルくれない？

B きのう、50ドルあげたばかりでしょ。そのお金はどうしたの。

A もう、使っちゃった。

B 金づかいが荒すぎるわ。金のなる木はないのよ。

153

61

Quit while you're ahead

proverb

勝っているうちにやめておけ

ことわざ

So long as you're winning, you should keep playing, right? After all, the more you play, the more you can win. The trouble is, you have to keep winning. You never know when your luck will run out. You might win the next game or you might lose. You might lose terribly and lose everything. It is safer to quit while you're ahead than to keep playing until you lose.

The time to quit an argument is when you are winning. If you keep fighting, you might find yourself on the losing side. The time to finish a relationship is before things get too ugly. If things don't get too ugly, you might be able to stay friends.

Everything we do in life is a gamble. We don't know how things will turn out in the end. It is important to look for signs that your luck might change. That is the time to think about making a decision—before it is too late.

勝っているうちは勝負を続けるべきですよね。何と言っても、勝負するほど、勝つことができるのですから。問題は、勝ち続けなければならないことです。運がいつ切れるかわかりません。次のゲームで勝つかもしれないし負けるかもしれない。ひどい負け方をして何もかも失うかもしれません。勝っているうちにやめるほうが、負けるまで勝負するよりも安全です。

議論した時は勝っているあいだにやめましょう。続けていたら、気がつくと負け組の側にいるかもしれません。人との関係は事態があまりにも見苦しくなる前に解消しましょう。そんなに見苦しくならなければ、友人でいられるかもしれません。

人生で行うすべてのことはギャンブルです。最後に事態がどうなるかなんてわかりません。大切なのは、運が変わる前兆を探すことです。その時こそ、手遅れにならないうちに、決断を考える時期です。

155

62

Don't bite the hand that feeds you

proverb

恩をあだで返すようなことはするな

ことわざ

If you depend on someone, don't treat that person badly. If you do, he or she may not support you anymore.

This proverb is a favorite of parents. When children get angry and shout at their parents, they are likely to hear their mom or dad say "don't bite the hand that feeds you."

This saying is not just for children, though. Adults depend on their jobs so they shouldn't say or do something unkind towards their bosses—at least not in front of them.

・・

誰かに頼っているなら、その人にひどい扱いをしてはなりません。そんなことをしたら、その人はもうあなたを助けてくれないかもしれません。

このことわざは親のお気に入りです。子どもが親に向かって腹を立てたり怒鳴りつけたりすれば、父親か母親に「恩をあだで返すようなことはするな」と言われるのが落ちでしょう。

けれども、このことわざは子ども以外にも通じます。大人は仕事をして生計を立てていますから、上司に向かって不親切なことを言ったりしたりしてはなりません——少なくとも目の前では。

157

63

People in glass houses shouldn't throw stones

proverb

ガラスの家に住む者は石を投げてはならない

ことわざ

A glass house is weak. Anyone can throw a stone and easily break it. If you live in a glass house, you don't want people to throw stones at you. If you throw a stone at someone else, then he or she is likely to throw a stone back at you. If that happens, your glass house will be in trouble. To protect yourself, you shouldn't start throwing stones.

Of course people don't live in glass houses; a glass house is too weak. However, people have many other weak points. We all have weak points. If you don't want someone to attack your weak points, then don't attack that person's weak points. The best way to protect yourself from getting hurt is to avoid hurting others.

ガラスの家は壊れやすい。誰でも石を投げて簡単に壊すことができます。あなたがガラスの家に住んでいるなら、誰かに石を投げつけられたくないでしょう。あなたが誰かに石を投げれば、その人は投げ返すかもしれません。そんなことになったら、ガラスの家は困ったことになります。自分を守るためには、石を投げてはなりません。

もちろん、ガラスの家に住んでいる人などいません。あまりにも壊れやすいからです。けれども、人にはほかにも多くの弱点があります。誰にだって弱点があります。誰かに自分の弱点を攻撃されたくなかったら、その人の弱点を攻撃するのをやめましょう。自分が傷つかないようにする最良の方法は、他者を傷つけないことです。

64

Don't burn your bridges behind you

proverb

渡った橋を燃やしてしまうな

ことわざ

If you burn the bridge to your past, you can never go back again. Everything you worked for will be lost to you forever.

Imagine you've been offered a new, better job. Finally, you will have the opportunity to work for a company that truly appreciates your talents. Your new job won't start until next month; until then, you'll keep working at your old job. Since you're leaving soon, there is no reason to keep working hard, right? Why not just take it easy for a few weeks?

Sure, a few easy weeks would be nice, but it's not a good idea. You need to keep working hard because you don't know what will happen in the future. Maybe something will go wrong at your new job. Someday you might want to go back to your old company. Someday you may find yourself working with the same people again. For this reason, you don't want to lose the trust of your old company and co-workers.

・・

過去につながる橋を燃やしたら、二度と戻れなくなります。努力してきたことすべてが永遠にあなたから失われるのです。

新しく、今より良い仕事の誘いがあったとしましょう。とうとう、あなたの才能を真に評価してくれる会社で働く機会ができるのです。新しい仕事が始まるのは来月です。それまで、元の職場で働くことになります。すぐにやめるのですから、一生懸命に働き続けなくてもよさそうですよね。どうして、数週間、のんびりしないのですか？

確かに、数週間のんびりとするのは楽でしょうが、いい考えではありません。一生懸命に働き続ける必要があるのは、将来何が起こるかわからないからです。もしかしたら、新しい職場で何か良くないことが起こるかもしれません。いつか元の会社に戻りたくなるかもしれません。いつかまた、同じ人たちと働くかもしれません。そんな理由から、あなたは元の会社や同僚の信頼を失いたくないのですね。

65

All that glitters is not gold

proverb

光るものすべてが金ではない

ことわざ

Just because something looks like gold doesn't mean it is gold. Things are not always what they appear to be. Something that appears to be wonderful may not be wonderful at all. Don't be easily fooled!

Fame is a good example. To many of us, fame is very attractive. Famous people wear beautiful clothes, travel around the world, and go to fancy parties. Given the choice, many of us would choose to be famous. However, famous people aren't always happy. They get lonely and sad, too. They might worry that their friends only like them because they are famous. If you start to think about it, fame doesn't sound like real "gold" at all.

何かが金のように見えたからって、それが金であるということではありません。物事は必ずしも見掛け通りではありません。すばらしく見えたものがまったくそうでないことがあります。簡単にだまされてはいけません。

わかりやすい例が名声です。多くの人にとって、名声はとても魅力があります。有名人は美しい衣装をまとい、世界中を旅し、きらびやかなパーティに出かけます。選べるものなら、多くの人は有名になることを選ぶでしょう。けれども、有名な人が必ずしも幸せであるとは限りません。孤独や悲しみを感じることもあります。友人が好意を示してくれるのは自分が有名だからではないかと心配するかもしれません。そんなことを考えると、名声はとても本物の「金」には見えなくなります。

66

Be careful what you wish for

proverb

願い事をする時は気をつけなさい

ことわざ

Here's the full sentence: "Be careful what you wish for, you might receive it." Since it is such a famous saying, people just say the first half because everyone knows how it ends.

"Be careful what you wish for" isn't just a famous proverb. It is also the opening line of a famous horror story*. In the story a man receives a strange object from an old friend. The friend tells him that the object has the power to make wishes come true. The man makes a wish and it comes true, but not exactly in the way he expected it to. In fact, the wish comes true in a horrible way.

The meaning of the story (and the proverb) is that a wish can be a dangerous thing. Sometimes the thing that you want turns out to be very different from what you imagined. Your wish might come true, but it might also bring you many problems that you didn't have before.

全文は「願い事をする時は気をつけなさい、かなうかもしれませんよ」です。とても有名なことわざなので、誰もが後半を知っているため、前半しか言いません。

「願い事をする時は気をつけなさい」は有名なことわざだけではなく、有名なホラー小説の冒頭でもあります。物語では、一人の男が旧友から奇妙な物を受け取ります。旧友は男に、これには願い事をかなえる力があると言います。男は願い事をしてかなえることができますが、予期していたものとはちょっと違う形でかないます。それどころか、願い事は恐ろしい形でかなうのです。

物語やことわざが意味するのは、願い事は危険なことがあるということです。時には願ったものが想像とかけ離れたものになることがあります。確かに願い事がかなうかもしれませんが、同時にこれまでになかった多くの問題が持ち上がるかもしれません。

*1992年からアメリカで出版された「グースバンプス」(R・L・スタイン著)のこと。

165

67

What goes around, comes around

proverb

因果は巡る
（自分の行いは自分に返ってくる）

ことわざ

If you spread gossip about other people, then other people are likely to spread gossip about you. If you hurt other people, then other people are likely to hurt you back. On the other hand, positive words and positive actions should create positive words and positive actions in return.

A Did you hear that Kate stopped talking to Amy?

B No. Why's that?

A Amy really made Kate angry by spending a lot of time with that guy whom Kate likes.

B But didn't Kate do the same thing to Emily a few months ago?

A I know. I don't feel sorry for Kate at all. *What goes around, comes around.* I hope she's learned her lesson!

ほかの人の悪口を広めると、その人たちもあなたの悪口を広めるかもしれません。ほかの人を傷つければ、その人たちもお返しにあなたを傷つけるかもしれません。これに反して、前向きな言葉や前向きな行動は、前向きな言葉と前向きな行動になって返ってきます。

A ケイトがエイミーと話すのをやめたって聞いた？

B いいえ。どういうこと？

A エイミーがケイトをかんかんに怒らせたの。ケイトの好きな男の子と長いこといっしょにいたせいよ。

B でも、ケイトだって数か月前、エミリーに同じことをしたじゃない。

A そうよ。ケイトがかわいそうだなんてまったく思わないわ。自分の行いは自分に返ってくるのよ。いい薬になるといいわね。

167

68

The devil is in the details

proverb

悪魔は細部に宿る

ことわざ

You've been offered a new job with higher pay. Sounds great, right? You had better check that contract carefully, though. Will you have to work weekends? How many vacation days will you get? How far is the office from your home and will the company pay for your gas or train fare? These small details can actually make a big difference. A great deal can start to look like a bad one once these details come to light.

This shouldn't be a surprise. Often these details are hidden on purpose to make a bad deal look good. That's where the word "devil" comes in; in Western culture, the devil is responsible for making the bad look good. Always check contracts and plans carefully, and when in doubt, ask questions!

あなたは給料の高い新しい仕事の誘いを受けました。すごいことですね。けれども契約書を注意深くチェックしたほうがいいですよ。週末に働くことになっていませんか。休暇は何日ありますか。家から職場までの距離はどのくらいで、ガソリン代や通勤コストは会社持ちですか。こんな小さな事柄が、実際には大きな違いになるのです。ひとたびこんな小さな事柄が明らかになると、すばらしく見えた待遇も悪く見えてきます。

これは驚くことではありません。このような小さな事柄は、悪い待遇を良く見せるために、わざと隠されていることが多いのです。ここで「悪魔」という言葉が登場します。西洋文化では、悪魔の役割は悪いものを良く見せることです。いつでも契約書や計画書を注意深くチェックして、疑問が出てきたら、質問をしてください！

69

If it ain't broke, don't fix it

Bert Lance, *politician (1931–2013)*

壊れていないものを修理するな

バート・ランス
政治家(1931〜2013)

Naturally, we want to make things better. Good is good until we get used to it. Good is good until it gets boring. We want our computers to do more. We want our businesses to earn more. We want our relationships to be more and more exciting. We want so badly to improve things that we forget to be happy that something actually works just fine the way it is.

Sometimes, by trying to make something better, people actually make something worse. A plan to grow a business can result in huge losses instead. A vacation designed to bring two people closer together can end in an argument. If something is working, leave it alone. Instead, put your energy towards the things in your life that really do need fixing.

当然ながら、人はものを良くしたいと思います。最初は良いものも、そのうち慣れてしまいます。最初は良いものも、だんだん退屈になります。人はコンピュータにもっとたくさんのことを要求するようになります。事業でもっと稼ぎたいと思います。人との関係がもっと心躍るものになることを望みます。人はあまりにも熱心にものを改善したいと思うため、物事が本来通り実際にうまくいっているのに、それでは満足できなくなるのです。

時には、人は何かを良くしようとして、実際には悪くしていることがあります。事業を拡大する計画が大きな損失を招くことがあります。二人を親密にしようと計画された休暇が口論で終わることがあります。物事がうまくいっているなら、そっとしておきなさい。その代わり、人生で本当に修理が必要なものにエネルギーを注いでください。

70

Never say never

proverb

絶対にない、ということはない

ことわざ

Anything can happen, so don't say that it won't. Of course this can be both a good thing and a bad thing. It's good when something you hoped for, but thought impossible, actually happens. Some good examples would be getting your dream job or finding the perfect partner. Never say never—these things can happen!

It's bad when something you weren't prepared for actually does happen. Just because something seems impossible doesn't mean that it is impossible. It is a good idea to prepare for anything, even the worst possible situation.

- **A** How was your date last night?
- **B** Terrible. I don't think I'll ever find the right man.
- **A** Hey, *never say never*! He's out there somewhere. You just have to keep looking.

どんなことでも起こる可能性があります。ですから、そんなことは起こらないと言ってはなりません。もちろん、これは良いことと悪いことのどちらにも当てはまります。うれしいのは、望んではいても不可能だと思っていたことが現実に起こった時です。その良い例が、夢見ていた仕事につけるとか、申し分のないパートナーに巡り会えることです。絶対にない、ということはないのです。このようなことが起こるのですから！

困るのは、準備できていないことが現実に起こった時です。あるものが不可能に見えるからといって、本当に不可能ではないのです。何事にも、最悪の状況になる可能性に対してさえも、準備しておくのは良い考えです。

- **A** ゆうべのデート、どうだった？
- **B** 最悪よ。いい人に会えるなんて無理な気がする。
- **A** ねえ、絶対にない、ということはないのよ。その人はどこかにいるわ。ただ探し続ければいいのよ。

173

71

Where there is smoke, there is fire

proverb

火のない所に煙は立たぬ

ことわざ

A bad sign, like smoke, is good evidence that a bad situation, like fire, is coming. Look out for warning signs and don't ignore them if you see them.

If you notice a small problem early, you may be able to keep it from growing into a larger problem. You will have time to prepare. If possible, you may even be able to avoid a bad situation completely. If you ignore the signs, however, you'll have no one to blame but yourself.

- A Something's not right at work. Nobody got a raise this year and a lot of people are quitting.

- B That doesn't sound good. *Where there's smoke, there's fire.* The company might be in trouble. I'd start looking for a new job, if I were you.

例えば煙のような悪い前兆は、火事などの悪い状況が起こることを示す十分な証拠になります。前兆に注意して、それを見つけたら無視してはなりません。

小さな問題も早く見つければ、大きな問題になるのを防ぐことができるかもしれません。準備する余裕も生まれます。もし可能なら、悪い状況を完全に避けることさえできるでしょう。けれども前兆を無視すると、自分を責めるしかなくなります。

- A 職場の様子が何かおかしい。今年は誰にも昇給がなかったし、たくさんの人がやめている。
- B どうもまずそうだな。「火のない所に煙は立たぬ」というからね。会社が面倒なことになっているのかもしれない。ぼくだったら新しい仕事を探すよ。

72

Don't put all your eggs in one basket

proverb

一つのことにすべてを賭けるな

ことわざ

If you put all your eggs in one basket, and the basket gets lost or stolen, you won't have any eggs left. It would be better to have your eggs in several baskets. Then if one gets stolen, you'll still have the eggs in the other baskets.

This proverb isn't really about eggs, though. It's about the choices we make and about preparing for the future. What happens if you can't get the job you want? What happens if you lose the job you have? Do you have other skills that you can use to make money? Where is your money? Is it invested in one place or many?

Life often doesn't go the way we want it to go. Life often doesn't go the way we expect it to go. It is important to prepare for many possible situations by having many "baskets."

もし持っている卵をすべて一つの籠に入れ、籠がなくなったり盗まれたりしたら、卵は一つも手元に残りません。いくつかの籠に卵を分けて入れるのが賢明でしょう。そうすれば、一つの籠が盗まれても、ほかの籠に卵が残ります。

もっとも、このことわざは何も卵についてばかりではありません。人々がする選択や、将来に対する備えについても言えます。希望の仕事につけなかったらどうなりますか。失業するとどうなりますか。ほかにお金を稼ぐための技能がありますか。お金はどこに預けていますか。投資先は一つですかそれともたくさんですか。

人生は望んだようにはならないことが多くあります。人生は予期したようにはならないことが多くあります。大切なのは、たくさんの「籠」を用意して、起こりそうな多くの状況に備えることです。

73

Better safe than sorry

proverb

転ばぬ先の杖

ことわざ

When you have a choice between a safe option and a risky option, choose the safe option. The risky option may look more attractive; however, if it doesn't work out, you could be in trouble. The safer option may look less attractive, but at least you won't have to worry about trouble. Few results are worth the risk of getting into trouble.

A I'm thinking of quitting my job.

B Do you have a new job lined up?

A No, not yet. But I think I should be able to find one. It would be nice to have some time off from working.

B I don't know. I think you should find a new job before you quit your old one. *Better safe than sorry*.

安全なほうか危険なほうかどちらかを選べと言われたら、安全なほうを選んでください。危険なほうが魅力的に見えるかもしれませんが、もしうまくいかなかったら、面倒なことになるかもしれません。安全なほうは魅力がないように見えるかもしれませんが、少なくとも面倒なことになる心配をしなくてすみます。面倒なことになる危険を冒してまで手に入れる価値がある結果などほとんどありません。

A 仕事をやめようと思う。

B 新しい仕事は決まったのかい？

A いやまだだ。でも見つけられると思うよ。しばらく仕事を休んでいられるのもいいな。

B そうかな。新しい仕事を見つけてから、今の仕事をやめるべきだと思うけどな。「転ばぬ先の杖」というだろ。

179

74

What you don't know can't hurt you

proverb

知らぬが仏

ことわざ

Sometimes it is better not to know something. Sometimes hearing something can cause pain. Sometimes it is better to hear no news than to hear bad news.

Bad news can make you feel bad, worried, or afraid. Bad news can change your life. If you don't hear bad news, then you won't feel bad. If nobody tells you something bad, then your life can stay the same.

The trouble with information is that once you know it, you can't stop knowing it. As long as you don't know, you can still hope for the best.

・・・

時には、知らないほうがいいことがあります。そのことを聞いたために苦しみが生まれることがあります。何もニュースを聞かないほうが悪いニュースを聞くよりいいことがあります。

悪いニュースを聞くと不安になったり、心配したり、恐ろしくなったりします。悪いニュースはあなたの人生を変えることがあります。悪いニュースを聞かなければ、不安になることもありません。誰もあなたに悪いことを伝えなければ、あなたの人生は変わりません。

情報の困った点は、ひとたび知ってしまうと、知ることを止められないことです。知りさえしなければ、今まで通り最善を望んでいられるのです。

Good Advice

Proverbs are part of the "cultural literacy" of each geographical region, country, and language. In childhood almost every Japanese learns certain proverbs, Americans learn certain proverbs, and the English learn certain proverbs. This "cultural literacy" is inherited by each new generation and becomes fundamental for belonging to that culture.

In this section, the good advice in the proverbs remains valid just about anywhere in the world.

We warn against expecting a business deal to be easily reached with "Don't count your chickens before they've hatched." We tell people that they have to endure harsh conditions if they want to succeed with "If you don't like the heat, get out of the kitchen." Kitchens are hot, tough working places and just as sports training camps are harsh environments, so you either have to get used to it or get out. We promote the following of a well-tested routine with "If it ain't broke, don't fix it."

良き助言

進化する「ことわざ」を使いこなす！

　ことわざとは、地理学的な地域、国、言語の「文化的な教養」の一部です。子どもの頃、ほとんどの日本人がある種のことわざを学ぶように、アメリカ人も、英国人もある種のことわざを学びます。この「文化的な教養」は各新世代によって受け継がれ、その文化に属するための基礎となるのです。

　本項では、ことわざで表される良いアドバイスは、世界中のどこにいようと今なお価値がある、ということを説明しています。

　商取引が容易に合意されることへの警告として、「捕らぬ狸の皮算用」という表現を用います。成功したいのなら辛い環境にでも耐えなければならないというときには、「暑いのが嫌なら厨房から出て行け」と表現します。厨房は暑く、骨の折れる職場であり、まさにスポーツのトレーニングキャンプのように過酷な環境なのです。そこでは、順応できなければ立ち去るしかないのです。十分にテストされた手順に従うことを勧めるのに、「壊れていないものを直すな」と表現します。

In negotiations as well as human relationships, something that can generally seem very easy may not be easy in reality. "The devil," we say, "is in the details." That is where the hard work is—not in the main points, but in the fine points. That is what takes time and energy to work out.

"Money doesn't grow on trees" may once have been used by parents toward their children who were always asking for money. But nowadays, a parent might be more likely to comment, "I am not an ATM!" to communicate the same message.

One proverb that is good advice for anyone who is undergoing a change in personal relationships would be advised to follow the advice "Don't burn your bridges behind you." The implication is that if you angrily break off a connection with someone, you may regret it. Because sometime in the future, you may need help from that person. The same holds in your career. No matter how happy you may be to leave certain people or duties behind, don't show your frustration or anger as you walk out the door. It is foolish to break off connections that you might need somewhere down the line. Just leave and close the door quietly behind you.

進化する「ことわざ」を使いこなす！

　交渉ごとや人間関係において、通常であれば非常に簡単に思えることが実は簡単にはいかないかもしれない、ということが起こります。これを「あらゆる細部に落とし穴は潜む」と言います。すなわち、大変な作業は、主要点についてではなく細部についてする作業なのです。細部を解決するには時間がかかり、エネルギーも必要なのです。

　「金のなる木はない」とは、いつもお小遣いを無心する子どもたちに向けて親たちが一度は使ったことがある表現かもしれません。しかし今日では、親であれば同じことを伝えるために、次のように言うことでしょう。「私はATMじゃありません！」

　人間関係を変えようとしている人にとっていいアドバイスになることわざとしては、このような表現が手助けになるのではないでしょうか——「背後の橋を燃やすな」。この表現は、もし怒りによって人間関係を壊すのなら、後悔することになりますよ、という意味を含みます。近い将来、その人に助けを求めることになるかもしれないからです。同じことがあなたのキャリアについても言えるのです。ある人たちや職務から解放されることがどんなに幸せであっても、ドアを出て行くときには不満や怒りを見せてはなりません。将来どこかで必要になるかもしれない関係性を断つなんて馬鹿げています。ただ、そっとドアを閉めて、立ち去ればいいのです。

Lessons
for Living

生きるための教訓

75

If life hands you a lemon, make lemonade

proverb

人生がレモンをくれるなら
それでレモネードを作ればいい
(つらい状況でも、ベストを尽くせ)

ことわざ

Make the best of your current situation, even if it is not the best situation. With a little creativity, you can turn something sour into something sweet. A little sugar and water are the only difference between lemons and lemonade.

Life gives us many examples of this. A blind child develops an excellent sense of hearing and later become a famous musician. A woman turns her painful divorce into a popular book that sells millions. Find the positive in the negative.

・・

現在の状況がたとえ最良の状況でなくても、最善を尽くしてください。少しばかりの創造力があれば、すっぱいものを甘いものに変えることができます。レモンに少しばかりの砂糖と水を加えるだけでレモネードができるのです。

人生にはこのような例がたくさんあります。盲目の子どもが聴覚をみがいて、後に有名な音楽家になりました。ある女性が苦しい離婚経験を本にして、それが評判になりミリオンセラーになりました。否定的なことのなかに肯定的なことを見つけてください。

76

Today is the first day of the rest of your life

Abbie Hoffman, *activist (1936–1989)*

今日は残りの人生最初の日である

アビー・ホフマン
活動家(1936～1989)

Do you wish you could change your life? Wouldn't it be nice to start again from the beginning?

Nobody can change the past. However, each day you can change the present. Look forward to the rest of your life. Don't look backwards to the part that you can't change. Yesterday may have been bad, but today can be good. What about the future? It can be great, but only if you start working on the present.

For hundreds of years, people have come to America from other countries to begin a new life. Because of this, Americans feel strongly that a fresh start is possible.

Actually, you don't need to move to have a fresh start; anyone can begin a new life anywhere. You just need to make a decision to start fresh. Try looking in the mirror and telling yourself: "Today is the first day of the rest of my life." Then start living the way you want to live.

自分の人生を変えることができたらいいのにと思いませんか。もう一度最初から始めるってすてきなことですよね。

誰も過去を変えることはできません。けれども、毎日、現在を変えることはできます。残りの人生に期待しましょう。変えることのできない過去を振り返らないでください。昨日は良くなかったかもしれないけれど、今日は良くなるかもしれない。では未来はどうでしょう？　きっとすばらしいでしょう。ただし、今日という日を頑張った場合に限ります。

何百年も前に、よその国から人々がアメリカにきて、新しい生活を始めました。このため、アメリカ人には新たに始めることができるという確信があります。

新たに始めるために、何も引っ越す必要はありません。誰でも新しい生活をどこででも始めることができます。新たに始めると決意するだけでいいのです。鏡をのぞいて自分に言い聞かせてください──「今日は残りの人生最初の日である」と。それから、自分の好きなように暮らし始めてください。

77

Don't sweat the small stuff

proverb

小さいことにくよくよするな

ことわざ

D on't worry about small problems. If you worry about every little thing, then you won't have enough strength left over to worry about the big problems. It is better to save your energy for when you really need it. More importantly, don't turn small problems into big ones. Stay calm and let things pass.

A Andy said he would call me yesterday, but he didn't. Do you think he doesn't like me? Should I call him?

B *Don't sweat the small stuff*. He was probably just busy. I'm sure he'll call you soon.

A And if he doesn't?

B Then forget about him! Just don't waste time and energy worrying about it, okay?

・・

小さな問題に悩まないでください。すべての小さなことに悩んでいたら、大きな問題に立ち向かうだけの強さがなくなってしまいます。本当に必要な時がくるまでエネルギーを節約するのが賢明です。もっと大切なことは、小さな問題を大きくしないことです。平静を保って物事をやり過ごしましょう。

A 昨日アンディが電話するって言ったのに、してこないの。わたしのこと好きじゃないのかな。こっちから電話しようかしら。

B 小さいことにくよくよしないで。たぶん忙しいだけよ。きっとすぐに電話してくるわよ。

A してこなかったら？

B その時は、彼のこと忘れなさい。そんなことでくよくよして時間とエネルギーを無駄にしちゃ駄目よ。

193

78

Truth is stranger than fiction

Mark Twain, *author (1835–1910)*

事実は小説よりも奇なり

マーク・トウェイン
作家(1835〜1910)

Books and movies often tell stories that are hard to believe. However, sometimes what happens in real life is even harder to believe. What happens in books and movies is limited to what the author can imagine. In real life, things can happen that we couldn't possibly imagine.

An actor becomes governor of a state. A man who never finished college runs one of the richest companies in the world. Someone puts a video on the Internet and becomes famous in just a few hours. Two people with the same name date the same person. Another gets married and divorced eight times. These things are hard to imagine but have all happened. Life is full of surprises!

・・・

本や映画では信じられないような話が語られることが多くあります。けれども、時には現実の世界で起こったことのほうがもっと信じがたいことがあります。本や映画で起こることは、あくまで作者が想像したことです。現実世界では、まったく想像もつかないことが起こることがあるのです。

俳優が州知事になり、大学を出ていない人が世界で最も裕福な会社の一つを経営しています。ある人はインターネットにビデオを流してほんの数時間で有名になりました。同姓同名の二人が同じ人とデートしました。ある人は結婚と離婚を8回繰り返しました。このようなことは想像しがたいですが、すべて実際に起こったことです。人生は驚きに満ちています！

79

Practice what you preach

proverb

人に説くことを自分でも実行しなさい

ことわざ

Follow your own advice. Doctors who tell their patients to exercise should exercise, too. Teachers who teach their students to work hard should work hard, too. If you don't follow your own advice, it is hard for others to take your advice seriously. You can't expect other people to listen to you if you don't listen to yourself. Be the kind of person who inspires other people.

A I heard the boss was sleeping during the meeting this morning.

B What? He's always getting angry with us for doing that. Why doesn't he *practice what he preaches*?

A Because he's the boss.

自分のした助言を実行しなさい。患者に運動を勧めた医者は自分も運動すべきです。生徒に一生懸命やれと教えた教師は自分も一生懸命やるべきです。あなたが自分のした助言を実行しなければ、人はあなたの助言を真剣に受け止めることはできません。自分自身の助言に耳を傾けなければ、人があなたに耳を傾けてくれることを期待できません。他者を奮い立たせられるような人になってください。

A 今朝、ボスが会議中に居眠りしていたらしいね。

B 何だって？　ぼくらがそんなことをしたらいつも腹を立てるのに。どうして人に説くことを自分でも実行しないんだろうね。

A そりゃあ、ボスだもの。

80

Every cloud has a silver lining

proverb

どんな悪い状況でも
どこかに希望があるものだ

ことわざ

Clouds block the sun and make the sky dark. Sometimes they bring rain that ruins our plans. However, if you look closely, you can see the light trying to break through around the edges. This part of the cloud isn't gray; it shines like silver.

In every bad situation, there is a small amount of good that shines through, just like the silver part of the cloud. Find this good and you can turn a negative situation into a positive one. You can turn an unhappy experience into a learning experience. The end of a romantic relationship, for example, can mean more time to spend with your friends.

Being positive takes practice. It isn't always easy to find the good when a situation seems so bad. Once you find it though, life looks a lot brighter.

・・・

雲は太陽をさえぎって、空を暗くします。時には雨をもたらして、わたしたちの計画をだいなしにします。けれども注意深く見つめると、雲間から光が差し込もうとしているのが見えてきます。雲のその部分は灰色ではありません。銀のように輝いています。

どんな悪い状況にも、ちょうど雲の銀色の部分のように、光が透き通って見える良い部分がわずかながらもあります。この良い部分を見つけられれば、暗い状況を明るい状況に変えることができます。不幸せな経験は学ぶべき人生経験になります。例えば、恋愛関係が終わった時には、友人たちと過ごす時間が増えたと考えればいいのです。

前向きになるには練習が必要です。状況がとても悪く見える時は、良い部分を見つけることは必ずしも簡単ではありません。けれども、ひとたびそれを見つけることができたら、人生はとっても明るくなります。

81

Either get busy living or get busy dying

Stephen King, *writer (1947–)*

精力的に生きるか、さもなくば 慌ただしく死んでいくか

スティーヴン・キング

作家(1947〜)

Sometimes it seems that life is just a pattern of getting up, going to work, eating dinner, watching television, and going back to bed. Is this really living? Shouldn't there be more excitement? Shouldn't there be more joy?

The good things in life don't always happen by themselves. Often, we have to make them happen. Get up early and watch the sunrise. Turn off the TV and take a walk in the park. Get busy doing what makes you happy. If you aren't busy doing the things that make you happy, what are you busy doing? If you don't take control of your life, someone else will—and before you know it, it will be gone.

・・・

時には人生が、朝起きて、仕事に行き、夕食を食べ、テレビを観て、ベッドに戻るというただの繰り返しに見えることがあります。これで生きていると言えるでしょうか。もっとわくわくすることはないのでしょうか。もっと喜びがないのでしょうか。

人生のすばらしい出来事は、必ずしも自然に起こるわけではありません。たいてい自分で起こさなくてはなりません。早く起きて朝日を見ましょう。テレビを消して公園に散歩に行きましょう。幸せな気持ちになることをして忙しく過ごしましょう。幸せな気持ちになることをして忙しく過ごさないなら、何をして忙しく過ごせと言うのでしょう。自分が人生の主導権を握らなければ、他人に握られます。そしてあっという間に人生は終わってしまうのです。

82

Beggars can't be choosers

proverb

背に腹は代えられぬ
（乞食はえり好みできない）

ことわざ

If you need to eat, you can't be picky about the food. Of course, a steak would be better than a slice of bread. But if you're hungry and a slice of bread is the only thing around, you won't say "no" to it. It's the same with jobs; you might want to wait for a better offer, but if you need to work, you'd better take what you can get.

This is advice for times when your luck is bad and few opportunities exist. Hopefully your luck will change and you won't be a "beggar" forever.

- A How's your new job?
- B Well, it's certainly not my dream job. But in this economy…
- A Yeah, I know what you mean. *Beggars can't be choosers*.

食べなければならない時、食べものをえり好みできません。もちろん、ステーキは一切れのパンよりいいでしょう。けれどもお腹がすいていて一切れのパンしかなければ、「いやだ」とは言えません。仕事についても同じです。もっといい仕事の誘いを待っていたいと思っても、働く必要があるなら、目の前のものを引き受けたほうがいいでしょう。

今言ったことは、あなたの運が悪くてほとんど機会がない時の助言です。うまくいけば運が変わり、いつまでも「乞食」でいることはないでしょう。

- A 新しい仕事はどう？
- B そうだな、決して夢見た仕事じゃないけれど、この景気じゃ……。
- A そうか、言いたいことはわかる。えり好みはできないからね。

83

In the future everyone will be world-famous for fifteen minutes

Andy Warhol, *artist (1928–1987)*

近い未来に、
誰もが世界中で15分間有名になるだろう

アンディ・ウォーホル
芸術家(1928～1987)

The artist Andy Warhol said this in 1968. He was saying that society was moving in a direction that would allow anybody—not just people with power—to be famous, if only for a short time.

Warhol didn't live to see the Internet; however, his words certainly seem to describe our present world. Today anybody can post something to the Internet and be famous, if only for a short time.

From this quote, we also get the popular saying "my fifteen minutes of fame." For example, you might hear someone say: "She's had her fifteen minutes of fame; when will it be my turn?"

There is no need to be jealous, though. Everyone can have a turn under the spotlight if they want it.

・・

芸術家のアンディ・ウォーホルがこれを言ったのは1968年です。彼が言ったのは、有力者に限らず誰もが、たとえ短時間であっても有名になれる方向に、社会が向かっているということです。

ウォーホルはインターネットを見ることなく亡くなりましたが、彼の言葉は確かに現在の世界について述べているように見えます。今日では誰もがインターネットに投稿して、たとえ短時間であっても有名になることができます。

この引用句から生まれたものに、「わたしも15分だけ有名人」という有名なことわざもあります。例えば、あなたは誰かがこう言うのを聞いたことがあるかもしれません──「彼女も15分だけ有名人になった。ぼくの番はいつくるのかな？」

けれども、焼きもちを焼く必要はありません。望みさえすれば、誰にでもスポットライトを浴びる番がやってきます。

84

You can't have your cake and eat it, too

proverb

ケーキは食べたらなくなる

ことわざ

If you eat your cake now, you'll have nothing for later. If you save your cake for later, you won't have it to eat now. There is no way to get around this. Once you eat the cake, it is gone forever!

The cake represents the good things in life. Sometimes it is not possible to have two good things at the same time. When this happens, you have to make a choice. It is a hard choice, but remember that either way you are getting a good thing.

  A How are things going with Lisa?
  B Great. We get along really well. The only thing is that I kind of miss being single. You know, going out and meeting new people…
  A So you're saying that *you want to eat your cake and have it too*?
  B If only that were possible!

・・

ケーキを今食べてしまうと、あとで食べることはできません。ケーキをあとに残しておくと、今食べることはできません。これを避ける道はありません。ケーキを食べてしまえば、永遠になくなるのです。

ケーキは人生のすばらしいものを表しています。時には、同時に二つのすばらしいものを手に入れられないことがあります。このような時、どちらかを選ばなくてはなりません。選ぶのは難しいですが、どちらにしても、すばらしいものが一つ手に入るということを忘れないでください。

  A リサとうまくいっているか？
  B もちろん。すごくうまくやっているよ。ただ一つ、独身でないことがちょっぴり寂しいだけさ。つまり、出かけて、初めての人に会ったりして……。
  A つまり、ケーキを食べても、なくならなければいいのにと言いたいんだろ？
  B それができたらいいのにな。

85

Wake up and smell the coffee

Ann Landers, *newspaper columnist (1918–2002)*

ちゃんと目を覚まして現実を見なさい

アン・ランダース
新聞コラムニスト(1918〜2002)

Breakfast in America usually starts with a big cup of coffee. The strong smell of coffee wakes up the senses, pulling people from their dreams and preparing them to face the day.

Do you have a friend who seems to live in a dream world? Does he or she often miss important signs? If you think your friend needs to pay more attention to the real world, you might want to remind him or her to "wake up and smell the coffee."

・・

アメリカの朝食は、たいてい大きなカップに入った一杯のコーヒーで始まります。コーヒーの強い香りが感覚を目覚めさせ、人々を夢の世界から引き出し、その日に立ち向かう準備をさせます。

夢の世界に住んでいるような友人はいませんか。その人は大切な兆候をしばしば見逃していませんか。もしあなたがその友人は現実の世界にもっと注意を払うべきだと思うなら、「ちゃんと目を覚まして現実を見る」ことを気づかせてあげたほうがいいかもしれません。

86

Better late than never

proverb

遅れても何もしないよりはまし

ことわざ

Naturally, we want things when we want them. We want food when we are hungry. We want an apology from a friend when he or she hurts us. We want a great job when we are looking for one. Of course, things don't always turn out the way we want. Sometimes what we want takes a lot longer to arrive than we would have liked. Instead of complaining about the timing, however, just be happy that you finally got what you wanted!

A My brother finally paid me back. It took him two years!

B Hey, *better late than never*. At least you got the money.

・・

当然ながら、欲しいものは欲しい時に手に入れたいものです。お腹がすいたら食べるものが欲しくなります。友人に傷つけられたらお詫びの言葉が欲しくなります。仕事を探していたらいい仕事が欲しくなります。もちろん、物事は思い通りにはいきません。時には、望んだよりずっとあとに欲しいものが手に入ることもあります。そんな時、遅くなったことに不平を言わず、欲しかったものがとうとう手に入ったことを喜んでください。

A 弟がようやくお金を返してくれた。2年もかかったよ。

B あのなあ、遅れても何もしないよりはましだろ。少なくともお金が返ってきたじゃないか。

87

Anyone who has never made a mistake has never tried anything new

Albert Einstein, *scientist (1879–1955)*

間違いを犯したことのない人は、新しいことに挑戦したことがない人だ

アルベルト・アインシュタイン

物理学者(1879〜1955)

If you try something new, you will probably make a mistake. This is only natural if you are doing something for the first time. It's okay to make mistakes in the beginning because this is how you learn. Sometimes it is necessary to make many mistakes before you get it right. That's okay, too. The important thing is to learn from the mistakes.

If you aren't making mistakes, then you aren't challenging yourself. A challenge can appear scary, but it doesn't need to be. A challenge is an opportunity to learn and gain new skills. Through challenges we can also gain experience and confidence. Ask yourself which is better: trying something new and making a mistake or never trying anything new at all?

・・

何か新しいことをしようとしたら、おそらく間違いを犯すでしょう。あなたがそれを初めてしたのなら、まったく当然なことです。最初に間違いを犯してもかまわないのです。それによって学ぶことができるからです。時には、正しく理解する前にたくさんの間違いを犯す必要がある場合もあります。それもかまいません。大切なのは、間違いから学ぶことです。

間違いを犯さないということは、あなたが挑戦していないということです。挑戦は恐ろしく見えるかもしれませんが、恐れる必要はありません。挑戦は新たな技能を学んで得る機会です。挑戦によって経験と自信も得られます。自分自身にどちらがいいか問いかけてください――何か新しいことに挑戦して間違いを犯すか、新しいことにまったく挑戦しないのかと。

88

What doesn't kill you only makes you stronger

proverb

生きてさえいれば
どんな経験でも自分自身を強くする

ことわざ

T o be alive is the most important thing in life. As long as you are alive, you can work on improving your situation.

With every difficult situation that you survive, you grow stronger. Most likely you are stronger than you realize! Situations that seemed terrible in the past may seem easier now because you have grown stronger. People who have lived through many terrible situations become very strong.

- **A** I can't believe he left me! What am I going to do? I have no job, no money…
- **B** It's terrible, I know! But you will be okay. You can't give up. Remember, *what doesn't kill you only makes you stronger*.
- **A** Well then, if I survive this, I'm going to be very strong. He'd better watch out!

....

生きているということは人生で最も大切なことです。生きてさえいれば、自分の状況を良くしようと励むことができます。

困難な状況を耐え抜くごとに、あなたは強くなります。まず間違いなく、自分で気づくより強くなっています。過去にはひどく見えた状況が今では簡単に見えるかもしれません。なぜなら、あなたが強くなったからです。ひどい状況をたくさん乗り越えてきた人は、とても強くなれるのです。

- **A** 彼がわたしを捨てるなんて信じられない。これからどうすればいいの。仕事もないしお金だって……。
- **B** ひどいわね。わかるわ。でもあなたなら大丈夫。あきらめては駄目よ。生きてさえいればどんな経験でも自分自身を強くすることを忘れないで。
- **A** それじゃ、これを耐えることができれば、強くなれるってわけね。彼は用心したほうがいいわね。

215

89

Showing up is 80 percent of life

Woody Allen, *filmmaker (1935–)*

顔見せは人生の80パーセント

ウディ・アレン
映画製作者(1935〜)

You may not be the best at what you do. You may not have been the smartest kid in the class or the fastest on the team. You may be completely ordinary and average. Don't feel bad about yourself! Being smart or fast can make you a success, but not if you can't get out of bed in the morning.

Ordinary skills, such as getting out of bed and getting dressed in the morning, really matter more than we think they do. Without these skills, nothing would get done! The simple act of showing up and getting to work on time is the starting point for everything else.

・・

あなたは自分のしていることで一番にはなれないかもしれません。クラスで一番賢かったり、チームで一番速く走れたりしたことがないかもしれません。あなたはまったく普通の平均的な人かもしれません。でも自分のことを嫌にならないでください。賢かったり、速く走れたりすると、成功者になれます。でも朝ベッドから起き出せなかったら、そうはいきません。

朝起きるとか着替えをするというような普通のことができるのは、考えているより、はるかに重要です。これができなければ、何もできないからです。顔を見せて時間通りに仕事を始めるという単純な行為は、ほかのすべてのことの出発点なのです。

90

There is no free lunch

Harley L. Lutz, *economist (1882–1975)*

ただより高いものはない

ハーレー・L・ルッツ

経済学者(1882〜1975)

Few gifts are true gifts; most have to be repaid at some point.

Be careful of the friend who invites you to lunch. She may ask you for a favor. Be careful of the neighbor who offers you the extra vegetables from his garden. Go over there to pick them up and you'll spend an hour listening to his problems. Be extra careful of the man who treats you to an expensive meal!

A free lunch may sound like a good idea, but remember that you'll likely have to pay for it some other way. Money is not the only currency and not always the most valuable one; time, energy, and attention can be just as valuable.

・・・

純粋な贈りものなどほとんどありません。たいていのものには、ある時点でお返しをしなければなりません。

ランチに招待してくれる友人に気をつけてください。彼女はあなたに何か頼むかもしれません。自分の庭のあまった野菜をくれる隣人に気をつけてください。隣家の庭に行って野菜を摘もうとすれば、隣人の問題を一時間聞かされるはめになるでしょう。高価な食事をおごってくれる人には特にご用心を！

ただでランチを食べられるのは良さそうに見えますが、別の方法で支払うことになるかもしれないことを忘れてはなりません。お金だけが唯一の通貨ではなく、必ずしも最も価値のあるものではありません。時間、精力、それに心づかいも同じように価値があるのです。

91

It doesn't rain but it pours

proverb

降れば土砂降り

ことわざ

When one bad thing happens, many bad things happen. Maybe this is true; maybe it isn't. However, it seems to be true! Bad luck seems to bring more bad luck. Or maybe it is just easier to see the bad—especially when something bad has just happened.

On the other hand, sometimes one good thing brings more good things. Sometimes it can bring more good things than you really want or need. Here's an example: John is looking for a job. Many months go by, but he still can't find a job. Suddenly he gets a job offer, then another, then another. Now he has too many job offers and has to make a difficult decision. In this situation John is probably thinking, "It doesn't rain but it pours."

・・・

悪いことが一つ起こると、続々と悪いことが起こります。これは本当かもしれません し、そうでないかもしれません。でも、やっぱり本当のようです。悪運はさ らに悪運をもたらすように見えます。あるいは、人はつい悪いほうばかり見てし まうのかもしれません——特に、何か悪いことが起こった直後はそうなります。

その一方で、時には一つの良いことが多くの良いことをもたらすことがあります。 時には実際に望んだり必要としたりするより多くの良いことをもたらすことがあ ります。例を挙げましょう。ジョンは仕事を探しています。数か月が過ぎてもま だ見つかりません。ある日突然、仕事の誘いがありました。それから次から次に 誘いがありました。今では誘いが多過ぎて、決めるのに苦労しています。このよ うな状況になって、ジョンはおそらく「降れば土砂降り」と思っているのでしょう。

92

A penny saved is a penny earned

Ben Franklin, *writer (1706–1790)*

ちりも積もれば山となる

ベンジャミン・フランクリン
文筆家(1706〜1790)

Saving a penny is the same as earning one. A penny is a penny; it doesn't make any difference to your wallet how it got there.

Of course, a penny doesn't sound like much money these days. Save a penny a day, and in a year, all you can buy yourself is a sandwich. However, start thinking about dollars and the numbers add up a lot quicker. Think about how small amounts of money quickly disappear—on taxi rides and cups of coffee, for example. Before spending money on these things, think about whether or not you really need them.

If you can save a few dollars every day, then in a year, you may be able to afford a vacation. Now that is something worth working for! What's more, the more money you save, the less you have to work for what you want.

・・・

１ペニーを節約することは１ペニー稼ぐことと同じです。１ペニーはしょせん１ペニー。どうやって手に入れようと、財布の中身はたいして変わりません。

もちろん今日では１ペニーは大金ではありません。一日に１ペニー節約したとしても一年後に買えるのはサンドイッチ一つです。けれどもドルだったら、金額はすぐに増えます。少額のお金が、例えばタクシー代や数杯のコーヒー代に、どれだけ早く消えてしまうか考えてください。このようなものにお金を使う前に、本当にそれが必要かどうか考えてください。

毎日、数ドル節約できるなら、一年後には休暇の資金ができるかもしれません。さあ、これはやってみる価値があることではありませんか！　その上、お金をたくさん節約するほど、そのぶん欲しいものを手に入れるために働かなくてすみます。

93

Control your own destiny, or someone else will

Jack Welch, *businessman (1935–)*

自らの運命をコントロールせよ。
さもなくば、他の誰かがそうするだろう

ジャック・ウェルチ
実業家(1935〜)

Life is full of choices. If you don't make them yourself, then somebody else will make them for you.

How many choices in your life have you made on your own? How many did you let others make? How many choices did you avoid making, because it was easier that way?

Making choices can be difficult. Sometimes there are too many options to choose from. Sometimes there aren't enough good options. Sometimes you don't want to feel responsible for making a difficult decision.

However difficult, making your own choices can put you in control of your own life. A sense of control can give you more confidence.

・・

人生には選択することがいっぱいあります。自分で選択しなければ、誰かがあなたの代わりに選択するでしょう。

人生で、何回自分で選択しましたか。何回他人に選択してもらいましたか。そのほうが楽だからといって、選択するのを何回避けましたか。

選択が難しい場合があります。時には選択肢が多過ぎることがあります。時には良い選択肢が十分にないことがあります。時には難しい選択をする責任を負いたくないと思うこともあります。

どんなに難しくても、自分で選択することで自分の人生をコントロールできるようになります。コントロールしているという感覚があなたの自信になります。

94

You don't need a weatherman to tell which way the wind blows

Bob Dylan, *musician (1941–)*

風がどの方向に吹いているのか知るために、
天気予報士は必要ない

ボブ・ディラン
ミュージシャン(1941〜)

You don't need an expert—or a machine!—to tell you what you can understand by yourself.

In the past, people used to tell time by checking the sun. Now we use clocks. That's not to say that clocks are bad; in fact, they're very useful for measuring time exactly. However, by using clocks, we've lost the ability to tell time by the sun. Most of us would probably turn on the TV to check the weather instead of opening the window.

Listen to your body. Your senses can tell you a lot more than you realize. What we learn in school and in books is only one kind of information. Real experience offers another kind of information that is just as valuable.

自分で理解できることを教えてもらうのに専門家や機械は、いりません。

昔は、人は太陽を観察して時間を知ったものです。現在では時計を使います。だからと言って時計が悪いというわけではありません。それどころか時計は時間を正確に測るのにとても役立ちます。けれども、時計を使うことで、人は太陽を見て時間を知る能力を失いました。ほとんどの人は、たぶん窓を開ける代わりにテレビをつけて天気を確かめているのでしょう。

あなたの体に耳を澄ましましょう。思っているよりずっとたくさんのことを感覚が教えてくれます。学校や本で学ぶことは、一種類の情報にすぎません。実際に経験することで、別の種類の情報が得られます。それは学校や本で学ぶ情報とまったく同じ価値があります。

95

When in Rome, do as the Romans do

proverb

郷に入っては郷に従え

ことわざ

When you travel outside your own culture, follow the customs of the local people. Follow the local customs even if these customs are different from your own. Eat something that you have never eaten before, even if it looks strange. Find out what the local people are excited about—a festival or a sports event maybe—and join in.

Trying new things is part of the experience of traveling. You may have the chance to try something that doesn't even exist in your culture. You might even discover that you like something that you didn't think you would. Sometimes you even get to do something that isn't allowed in your own culture.

文化の違う土地に旅行する時は、地元の人の習慣に従いなさい。それが自分の土地の文化と違っても、地元の習慣に従いなさい。たとえそれが奇妙に見えても、これまで食べたことのないものを食べなさい。地元の人が何に興奮するか——たぶん、お祭りやスポーツ大会でしょう——見つけて、それに参加しなさい。

新しいことに挑戦するのは、旅行経験の一部です。自分の土地の文化には存在さえしないことに挑戦する機会があるかもしれません。好きになれるとは思わなかったものが好きなことに気づくことさえあるでしょう。時には、自分の土地の文化では許されていないことができることさえあります。

96

The only thing we have to fear is fear itself

Franklin D. Roosevelt, *President (1882–1945)*

私たちが恐れなければならない唯一のことは、恐れそのものである

フランクリン・デラノ・ルーズベルト

大統領(1882〜1945)

Roosevelt said this famous line in 1933. At the time, the economy in America was very bad. People were afraid. They were afraid of losing their jobs. If they had already lost their jobs, they were worried about losing their homes. They were afraid that things would never get better.

People had good reasons to be afraid. Maybe the economy would only get worse; on the other hand, maybe it would get better. It is important to stay positive and hope for the best. Without hope, it is impossible to imagine a better future. Fear destroys this hope and that is why it is dangerous. Fight back against fear with positive thinking.

ルーズベルトがこの有名なせりふを言ったのは1933年です。そのころアメリカ経済はひどく悪化していました。人々は恐れていました。仕事を失うことを恐れました。すでに仕事を失った人々は家を失うことを恐れました。人々は物事が決して良くならないのではないかと恐れました。

人々には恐れるだけの理由がありました。経済は悪化の一途をたどるのかもしれません。これに反して、どんどん良くなるのかもしれません。大切なのは常に前向きでいて、最善を望むことです。希望がなければ、良い未来を想像することはできません。恐怖はこの希望を打ち砕くので、危険なのです。前向きな思考で恐怖を克服しましょう。

97

Do a common thing in an uncommon way

Booker T. Washington, *educator & author (1856–1915)*

普通ではない方法で普通のことをするのは すばらしいこと

ブッカー・T・ワシントン
教育者・作家(1856〜1915)

Every day millions of people on Earth do the same things. We get up in the morning, eat breakfast, go to work, and so on. Often, we do the same thing the same way that our parents did and that their parents did before them. We do so many of these common things without even thinking about how or why we do them. We do so many things without thinking that there might be a different or better way to do them.

Since these are things that you do every day, doing just one of those things differently can make a big difference in your life. What's more, doing an ordinary thing in a different way can make people notice you. Doing an ordinary thing in a better way can earn you respect.

毎日、地球上の何百万もの人々が同じことをしています。朝起きて、朝食を食べ、仕事に行くなどです。しばしば、人は親がしたのと同じやり方で同じことをしています。親はそのまた親の通りにしています。人はそんなに多くの普通のことを、どのように、なぜするのか考えることさえなく繰り返しています。人はそんなに多くのことを、違ったやり方やもっといいやり方がほかにあるかもしれないと考えもせず繰り返しています。

このようなことは毎日することですから、どれか一つでも別の方法でやれば、人生に大きな違いをもたらすかもしれません。その上、普通のことを別の方法でやれば、注目を集めます。普通のことをもっといい方法でやれば、尊敬を得られます。

98

Reality is something you rise above

Liza Minnelli, *actress & singer (1946–)*

現実とは踏み越えていくもの

ライザ・ミネリ
女優・歌手(1946〜)

Reality is what life gives you. You may have been born male or female, tall or short. You may stay healthy or you may get sick. Reality is not always what we would choose, if we had the choice.

However, what you choose to do with what life gives you is up to you. You can choose to accept reality or you can choose to ignore reality. You can also choose to make the best of it.

Reality is only the starting point. See how far you can go from there. Learn to tell the difference between what you think is impossible, what other people tell you is impossible, and what really is impossible.

・・

現実とは人生が与えてくれたものです。あなたは男に生まれたかもしれないし女に生まれたかもしれない。背が高く生まれたかもしれないし低く生まれたかもしれない。健康でいられるかもしれないし病気になるかもしれない。現実とは、たとえ選ぶことができたとしても、必ずしも選んだようにはなりません。

けれども、人生が与えてくれたものとどのようにつきあうか選ぶのは、あなた自身です。現実を受け入れることを選んでもいいし、無視することを選んでもいいのです。現実を最大限に生かすことを選ぶこともできます。

現実は出発点にすぎません。そこからどれだけ遠くまで行けるか見てください。自分が不可能だと考えたもの、人があなたに不可能だと言ったもの、そして本当に不可能なものの違いがわかるようになってください。

99

There's no place like home

John Howard Payne, *actor & playwright (1791–1852)*

わが家にまさるところなし

ジョン・ハワード・ペイン
俳優・劇作家(1791〜1852)

This is one of the most famous lines from one of the most famous American movies. The movie is "The Wizard of Oz," which was based on the book by L. Frank Baum.

In the story, the main character is taken to a world far away from her home. There are many wonderful things in this world, and she makes some good friends there. However, she really wants to go home, even though her home is just an ordinary home in an ordinary place. Why does she want to go home so badly? Because no place, no matter how wonderful, is as special as home. To get home, she must repeat the words, "There's no place like home."

Maybe you feel the same way after returning home from a holiday. Even though you had a wonderful time, it feels so good to be back in your own house. You open the door, put your bags down, take off your shoes, and think, "There's no place like home!"

これは最も有名なアメリカ映画の一つで言われた最も有名なせりふの一つです。映画は『オズの魔法使い』で、原作はライマン・フランク・ボームの本です。

物語では、主人公の女の子が家から遠く離れた世界に運ばれます。その世界にはすばらしいものがあふれ、すてきな友だちもできます。それでも女の子は、普通の場所にある本当に普通の家なのに、家に帰りたくてたまりません。どうしてそれほどまでに帰りたいのでしょう？　なぜなら、どんなにすばらしくても家ほど大切なところはないからです。家に戻るために、女の子は「わが家にまさるところなし」という言葉を何回も唱えなければなりませんでした。

あなたも休暇から家に帰ったら同じように感じるかもしれませんね。どんなにすばらしい時間を過ごしたとしても、自分の家に帰るとほっとします。玄関の戸を開けて、かばんを置いて、靴をぬいで思うのです。「わが家にまさるところなし」と。

100

The best things in life are free

proverb

**人生で最も大切なものは、
いくらお金を出しても手に入らない**

ことわざ

Make a list of all of the things that make you happy. How many of the things on that list can be bought? How many of them can't be bought? How many of them are expensive? How many of them are free?

Sure, expensive things can make you happy. However, unless you're rich, you'll have to work hard to be able to buy them. If you need expensive things to be happy, you'll have to work hard your whole life to be happy.

Some important things you can't buy, like love for example. Other examples are a sunny day, a walk in the park, and an afternoon with friends. You can't buy these things, but they can make you just as happy—even happier—than something you can buy. The easiest way to be happy is to enjoy these little free things.

あなたを幸せにしてくれるもののリストをつくってみてください。リストのなかで買えるものはいくつありますか。買えないものはいくつありますか。高価なものはいくつありますか。ただのものはいくつありますか。

確かに、高価なものは幸せな気持ちにしてくれます。けれども、お金持ちでない限り、それを得るために必死で働かなくてはなりません。幸せな気持ちになるために高価なものが欲しいなら、そのために一生、必死に働かなくてはならないでしょう。

例えば愛のように、お金で買えない大切なものがいくつかあります。ほかにも、ぽかぽかとお日様の照る日、公園の散歩、友人たちと過ごす午後などがあります。このようなものはお金では買えませんが、買えるものと同じくらい、いえ、もっともっと幸せな気持ちにしてくれます。幸せになる一番簡単な方法は、このようなささやかでお金のかからないものを楽しむことです。

Lessons for Living

One of the most common of all English proverbs is "When in Rome…" It is so common that people don't even have to say the second phrase, because the first is sufficient to convey the whole message. To freshen up the proverb and put your own spin on it, why not switch the city and say "When in Osaka…". The initial "When in…" is unique enough that the other person will recognize what you are saying, so you can play with the city name. This is the kind of playfulness that help proverbs stay relevant.

Parents have long told their children that "showing up is 80 percent of life." Each parent has his or her own variation, including raising the percentage to 90 percent and replacing "life" with "success" or "winning". All of these variations have a ring of truth to them. In other words, you can't do anything well if you don't try. The same message is conveyed by "Anyone who has never made a mistake has never tried anything new." This is the basic idea behind "disruption" which is so often in the news these days referring to new types of businesses, especially IT

生きるための教訓

進化する「ことわざ」を使いこなす!

すべての英語のことわざの中でもっともよく知られたものの一つに「ローマにおいては……」というのがあります。あまりにもよく使われるので、2番目のフレーズはいう必要さえありません。というのも、最初のフレーズだけで、すべての意味合いを伝えるには十分だからです。このことわざを新鮮な言い方で一捻りして、「大阪においては……」などと言うことができます。出だしの「〜においては」という表現は非常に独特なので、誰もが言わんとすることを理解してくれることでしょう。だから、街の名前で遊べます。このような言葉遊びは、ことわざを身近なものにしてくれます。

親は子どもにいつも「参加することは人生の80％だ」と言いつづけてきました。親によってそれぞれの言い回しを持っています。数字を90％に上げたりとか、「人生」を「成功」や「勝利」に置き換えたりしています。こういった言い回しはすべて、子どもたちにとっては真実なのです。つまり、挑戦しない限り、なにごとも成し遂げられないのです。同じようなメッセージを「過ちを犯したことのない者は、新しいことに挑んだことがない」と伝えることもできます。この表現は、最近の報道でよく使われる「破壊」ということばの背後にある基本的な概念なのですが、すっかり伝統産業に取って代わった新しいビジネス形態、特にIT企業について言及するときに使

companies, that completely supercede traditional industries. Examples of these "disrupters" are the driverless vehicle, which may someday replace drivers of taxis and trucks and 3D printers, which eliminate many stages of manufacturing.

People who are faced with difficult negotiation with others, in private life and business life, would do well to consider the wisdom of "Don't sweat the small stuff." That is, the fine details came come later, after you have a basic agreement worked out. And the proverb "There is no free lunch" reminds us that nothing in life is "free." Someone has to pay for it.

Some very memorable quotations are based on proverbs. Surely one of the sharpest observations is from the fashion designer Coco Chanel. She is reputed to have said, "The best things in life are free. The second-best things are very, very expensive." Chanel was astute as a designer and as a commentator on life in general.

進化する「ことわざ」を使いこなす!

われています。こういった「破壊者」の例としては、いつの日かタクシーやトラックの運転手に取って代わる自動運転車や生産過程の多くを削除する3Dプリンターを挙げることができます。

個人的な生活やビジネスの場において、他人との困難な交渉に直面したことのある人は、「小さなことにくよくよするな」という賢明な教えについて、考えたほうがよいでしょう。つまり、最後の詰めは、基本的な契約が交わされた後になされるということです。また、「タダより高いものはない」ということわざは、世の中に「タダ」のものなんか何もない、ということを思い起こさせてくれます。誰かが支払わなければならないのです。

非常に記憶に残っている引用文のなかには、ことわざを元にしたものがあります。間違いなく、もっとも鋭い観察力に裏打ちされたことばはファッションデザイナーのココ・シャネルが発したものでしょう。彼女は「人生で最高のものはタダよ。2番目にいいものは、とっても、と〜っても、高いの」と言って評判になりました。シャネルはデザイナーとしても、人生一般のコメンテーターとしても洞察力が深かったのですね。

格言の著者

(頭の数字は、該当する格言の番号です。)

1

Ralph Waldo Emerson *(1803–1882)* ラルフ・ワルド・エマーソン

ハーバード大学を卒業後は神学校で学び、牧師の資格をとる。代表作に『自然論』『偉人論』など。「あなた以外にあなたに平和をもたらすものはいない」などの言葉がある。

3, 20, 92

Ben Franklin *(1706–1790)* ベンジャミン・フランクリン

アメリカ独立に、政治家として貢献した。ビジネスマンとして成功した後、自然科学の発明にも貢献。現在の100ドル紙幣に肖像が描かれている。「信用は金なり」とも言っている。

6

Yogi Berra *(1925–2015)* ヨギ・ベラ

メジャーリーグのヤンキースで活躍したプロ野球選手。背番号8は永久欠番になっている。ユーモアあふれる発言で、今でもアメリカ人に親しまれている。

9

Joseph P. Kennedy *(1888–1969)* ジョセフ・P・ケネディ

合衆国史上最も若く、かつ初のカトリック教徒として大統領となったJ・F・ケネディの父として知られるが、本人も民主党の大物政治家だった。金融業、映画会社、スコッチの輸入などで財を成した。

12

Frank Leahy *(1908–1973)* フランク・リーヒー

アメリカン・フットボールの選手。ボストン大学、ノートルダム大学でコーチとして活躍。

13

Herman Edwards *(1954–)* ハーマン・エドワーズ

フィラデルフィアのアメリカン・フットボールチーム、イーグルスで10年間、コーナーバックとして活躍。ニューヨーク・ジェッツのヘッドコーチも務める。

15

Thomas Edison *(1847–1931)* トーマス・エジソン

生涯の発明は1300にのぼるといわれるアメリカの発明王。電話機、蓄音機などの発明は誰もが知っているところ。GE社の設立者としても有名。

17

Dale Carnegie *(1888–1955)* デール・カーネギー

ミズーリ州出身の実業家、著述家、ビジネスセミナー講師。大学卒業後に新聞記者、俳優、セールスパーソンなどを経てD・カーネギー研究所を設立。世界的ベストセラー『人を

動かす』の著者として有名。

22

Walt Disney *(1901–1966)* ウォルト・ディズニー

誰もが知る「ミッキーマウス」や「ディズニーランド」の生みの親。一族はアイルランドからの移民。幼少期から絵を描くのが好きで、一生夢を追い続けた。他の言葉に、「不可能なことは何もない」

25

Daniel Webster *(1782–1852)* ダニエル・ウェブスター

アメリカの政治家、法律家。貧しい農家の生まれだが、教育熱心だった両親のおかげで、ダートマス大学を卒業、弁護士としても活躍。

29, 33

Eleanor Roosevelt *(1884–1962)* エレノア・ルーズベルト

アメリカ第32代大統領フランクリン・ルーズベルトのファーストレディーとしてよく知られている。国連のアメリカ代表も務め、数々の名言を残している。

36, 54

Abraham Lincoln *(1809–1865)* エイブラハム・リンカーン

アメリカ国民に最も愛された大統領の一人。ケンタッキー州の貧しい農家で生まれ、独学で法律を学んだ。「奴隷解放の父」とも称される。

41

Jimi Hendrix *(1942–1970)* ジミ・ヘンドリックス

日本では「ジミヘン」と呼ばれて愛された、アメリカのミュージシャン。黒人の父、インディアンの母との間にシアトルで生まれる。天才的なギターテクニックで、ミュージシャンに大きな影響を与えた。

45

Billy Wilder *(1906–2002)* ビリー・ワイルダー

オーストリア出身の新聞記者、脚本家。ユダヤ人であったため、ナチの台頭とともにメキシコを経てアメリカに移民。『お熱いのがお好き』『アパートの鍵貸します』などの脚本で有名。

48

Leo Durocher *(1906–1991)* レオ・ドローチャー

マサチューセッツ州生まれの野球選手。ヤンキース、ドジャースの選手として活躍した後、監督になり、通算2008勝を記録している。

51

Dr. Seuss *(1904–1991)* ドクター・スース

マサチューセッツ州生まれの絵本作家。現代のマザー・グースとも言われる、代表作『The Cat in the Hat』は、世界中の子供に愛されている。

56
Muhammad Ali *(1942–)* モハメド・アリ

ケンタッキー州生まれのボクシングの元世界チャンピオン。本名、カシアス・クレイ。1960年のオリンピックで金メダルをとったが、当時のアメリカ社会は、まだ黒人差別が激しく、祝賀ムードもなかったという。怒った彼は、金メダルを川に投げ捨てたという逸話もある。

69
Bert Lance *(1931–2013)* バート・ランス

アメリカの実業家であり、カーター政権の行政管理予算局長。「壊れていないものを修理するな」は、1977年の雑誌『Nation's Business』に掲載された言葉。

76
Abbie Hoffman *(1936–1989)* アビー・ホフマン

ユダヤ人家庭に生まれ、マサチューセッツ州で育つ。政治活動家。1968年にはベトナム反戦を訴え、逮捕された経歴を持つ。

78
Mark Twain *(1835–1910)* マーク・トウェイン

『トム・ソーヤーの冒険』などで知られるアメリカの作家。数多くの小説、エッセーを世に送り出した。「これまで思い悩んだことのうち、98パーセントは取り越し苦労だった」なども彼の言葉。

81
Stephen King *(1947–)* スティーヴン・キング

「モダン・ホラーの旗手」とも呼ばれるアメリカの人気作家。彼の作品は次々とベストセラーになり、世界中で翻訳、また映画化されている。

83
Andy Warhol *(1928–1987)* アンディ・ウォーホル

アメリカの画家、芸術家。両親はチェコスロバキアからの移民。キャンベル・スープの缶をモチーフにするなど、ポップアートの生みの親として知られる。

85
Ann Landers *(1918–2002)* アン・ランダース

専業主婦・母だったイッピー・レダラー（本名）は、シカゴ・サンタイムズの「Ask Ann Landers」というコラムを任されることになる。以来、アン・ランダースとして読者からの数々の質問に答え続けた名物コラムニスト。

87
Albert Einstein *(1879–1955)* アルベルト・アインシュタイン

ドイツ生まれのユダヤ人。相対性理論、ブラウン運動など数々の業績を残した物理学者。偉大な学者にも関わらず、「自分は天才ではなく、ただ一つのことをやり続けただけだ」と言っている。

89

Woody Allen (1935 –) ウディ・アレン

大学時代から新聞、雑誌にジョークなどを投稿していたというユーモアセンスあふれる映画監督、俳優。アカデミー監督賞、脚本賞を受賞するも、式には出ないなどハリウッドには背を向けた人としても有名。

90

Harley L. Lutz (1882–1975) ハーレー・L・ルッツ

国家財政、税金についての研究に生涯をかけた経済学者。政府の歳出が増加することに対して、厳しく批判した。

93

Jack Welch (1935 –) ジャック・ウェルチ

1981年から20年間、ゼネラル・エレクトリックのCEOを務めたアメリカの実業家。『フォーチュン』誌で、20世紀最高の経営者にも選ばれたことがある。

94

Bob Dylan (1941–) ボブ・ディラン

アメリカ公民権賛同歌として知られる「風に吹かれて」の作者、ミュージシャン。メッセージ性の強い楽曲を数多く残し、アメリカ音楽界にも多大な影響を与えてきた。

96

Franklin D. Roosevelt (1882–1945) フランクリン・デラノ・ルーズベルト

ニューヨークの裕福な地主の家に生まれる。第32代アメリカ大統領。史上唯一、4選を果たした大統領として知られる。経済立て直しのためニューディール政策を推進したことで知られる。

97

Booker T. Washington (1856–1915) ブッカー・T・ワシントン

奴隷として生まれた彼は、南北戦争後にようやく自由を得、学校に通うようになる。後に有名な教育者となり、黒人のための高等教育機関を設立した。黒人として、アメリカ史上初めて、切手のモデルに採用された。

98

Liza Minnelli (1946 –) ライザ・ミネリ

わずか2歳で映画デビューしたというアメリカの女優で歌手。アルコール依存症、難病などを克服し、その度に第一線にカムバックした。ブロードウェイミュージカル、映画など多数の作品に出演。

99

John Howard Payne (1791–1852) ジョン・ハワード・ペイン

アメリカ生まれの俳優、詩人、劇作家。イギリスで初めて活躍した役者とも言われる。「わが家にまさるところなし」は彼が作詞したイングランド民謡「Home! Sweet Home!（埴生の宿）」の中の一節。

日英対訳
ビジネスで使える英語のことわざ・名言100
Inspirational Proverbs and Sayings for Business

2016年7月8日　第1刷発行

著　者　レベッカ・ミルナー
解　説　ジェームス・M・バーダマン

発行者　浦　晋亮

発行所　IBCパブリッシング株式会社
　　　　〒107-0051 東京都新宿区中里町29番3号
　　　　菱秀神楽坂ビル9F
　　　　Tel. 03-3513-4511　Fax. 03-3513-4512
　　　　www.ibcpub.co.jp

印刷所　株式会社シナノパブリッシングプレス

© 2016 IBC Publishing
Printed in Japan

落丁本・乱丁本は、小社宛にお送りください。送料小社負担にてお取り替えいたします。
本書の無断複写（コピー）は著作権法上での例外を除き禁じられています。

ISBN978-4-7946-0417-0